*Make
Every Day
Count*

Make Every Day Count

previously published as
Every Day Deserves a Chance

MAX LUCADO

THOMAS NELSON
Since 1798

NASHVILLE   DALLAS   MEXICO CITY   RIO DE JANEIRO

ISBN 978-1-4003-1822-3 (2012 edition)

Library of Congress Cataloging-in-Publication Data

Lucado, Max.
[Every day deserves a chance]
Make every day count / Max Lucado.
p. cm.
"Previously published as Every day deserves a chance: teen edition"--T.p. verso.
Includes bibliographical references.
ISBN 978-1-4003-1822-3 (pbk.)
1. Christian teenagers--Religious life. I. Title.
BV4531.3.L8 2012
248.8'3--dc23
2011030001

Printed in the United States of America
12 13 14 15 QG 6 5 4 3 1

For Steve and Annie Millett—
thanking God for the way you bring
life to San Antonio youth.

Contents

Acknowledgments

Great thanks to these folks who poured their skill and hard work into this book:

Karen Hill, Laura Minchew, Amy Parker, Rhonda Hogan, John McPherson, Kay Meadows, Julie White, Kevin Harvey, Shana Bell, Shannon Whitehead, Rob Birkhead, Michelle Prater Burke, and Jennifer Barrow.

CHAPTER 1

Make Every Day Count

This is going to be a great day! I thought, sitting on the beach listening to the waves and feeling the warm sun. I took a deep breath, leaned back in the beach chair, and closed my eyes.

That's when a bird chose my chest for target practice. No warning. No sirens. No, "Bombs away!" Just *plop*.

I looked up just in time to see a seagull giving high feathers to his bird buddies on the branch. Yuck. I poured water on my shirt three times. I moved to a chair away from the trees. I did all I could to regain the magic of the morning, but I couldn't get my mind off the bird flyby.

It should have been easy. Waves still rolled. Clouds still floated. The ocean lost no blue; the sand lost no white.

Palm trees still swayed, and wind still whispered. But I couldn't quit thinking about the seagull grenade.

Stupid bird.

Birds have a way of messing things up, don't they? Count on it: into every day a bird will plop.

Parents will argue.

Teachers will correct.

Bullies will taunt.

Friends will forget.

And lines. Oh, the lines. Missed goal lines, flubbed play lines, long lines, deadlines . . .

Each day brings with it disappointments and demands.

And what about those days of double shadows? Those days when hope is blasted by crisis? Days of hospitals and wheelchairs, sickness and sorrow. You wake up in the same scary neighborhood or abusive household. The failing report card is still folded in your pocket, the head of the dinner table still empty, the cemetery dirt still fresh. Who has a good day on *these* days?

Most don't . . . but wait—couldn't we try? Doesn't even the worst of days deserve an opportunity? A shot. A try-out. An audition. A swing at the plate. Doesn't every day deserve a chance to count for something?

After all, "this is the day the Lord has made; we will rejoice and be glad in it" (Psalm 118:24 NKJV). The first word in the verse leaves us scratching our heads. "*This* is the day the Lord has made"? Perhaps holidays are the days the Lord has made. Saturdays are the days the Lord has made. Easter Sundays . . . birthdays . . . vacation days— these are the days the Lord has made. But "*this* is the day"?

"This is the day" includes every day. Breakup days, final exam days, moving days, being grounded days. Sending-your-firstborn-off-to-college days.

{"This is the day" includes every day.}

That last one sucked the starch out of my shirt. Surprisingly so. We packed Jenna's stuff, loaded up her car, and left life as we'd known it for eighteen years. A chapter was closing. One less plate on the table, voice in the house, and child beneath the roof. The day was necessary. The day was planned. But the day undid me.

I was a mess. I drove away from the gas station with the nozzle still in my tank, yanking the hose right off the pump. Got lost in a one-intersection town. We drove; I moped. We unpacked; I swallowed throat lumps. We filled the dorm room; I plotted to kidnap my own daughter and take her home where she belongs. Did someone store my chest in dry ice? Then I saw the verse. Some angel had tacked it to a dormitory bulletin board.

This is the day the LORD has made;
We will rejoice and be glad in it.

I stopped, stared, and let the words sink in. God made this day, ordained this hard hour, designed the details of this wrenching moment. He isn't on holiday. He still holds the conductor's baton, sits in the cockpit, and occupies the universe's only throne. Each day emerges from God's drawing room. Including this one.

So I decided to give the day a chance, change my view, and imitate the resolve of the psalmist: "I will rejoice and be glad in it."

Oops, another word we'd like to edit: *in*. Perhaps we could swap it for *after*? We'll be glad after the day. Or *through*. We'll be glad to get through the day. *Over* would work. I'll rejoice when this day is over.

But rejoice *in* it? God invites us to. As Paul rejoiced *in* prison; David wrote psalms *in* the wilderness; Jonah prayed *in* the fish belly; Paul and Silas sang *in* jail; Shadrach, Meshach, and Abednego remained resolute *in* the fiery furnace; John saw heaven *in* his exile; and Jesus prayed *in* his garden of pain . . . Could we rejoice smack-dab *in* the midst of this day?

Imagine the difference if we could.

Suppose neck-deep in a "terrible, horrible, no good, very bad day,"[1] you resolve to make this day count anyway. You choose not to whine or worry or sleep it away but to give it a fair shake. You trust more. Stress less. Amplify gratitude. Mute grumbling. And what do you know? Before long the day is done and surprisingly decent.

So decent, in fact, that you resolve to make the next day count too. It arrives with its hang-ups and bang-ups, bird drops and shirt stains, but for the most part, by golly, choosing to make your day matter works! So you do the same the next day and the next. Days become weeks. Weeks become months. Months become years of good days.

A few years ago, Nathan Burditt started with one

MAKE EVERY DAY COUNT

decision one day to give one thing—one pretty cool thing—
and is changing the days and lives of others, as well as his
own.

NEW HAMPSHIRE UNION LEADER

Teen's Gift Surprises, Inspires

By John Whitson,
staff writer

Nathan Burditt waited 34
hours outside a Target store
in Hooksett last week to buy
a Sony PlayStation 3 gaming
machine.

His patience paid off when
he was able to get the scarce
$600 device.

Then he gave it away.

"It felt good. It still feels
good," said the Memorial High
School senior yesterday.

The PlayStation 3 went to
help fellow Memorial students
who Burditt had never heard of
before this week. In fact, Burditt
would probably be spending
part of this Thanksgiving Day

learning the nuances of his new
prized possession if it weren't
for Christine Monahan. The
civics and history teacher has
been busy recently helping
students organize a fundraiser
to benefit the Hudon family.

Stephanie Hudon is
a 15-year-old freshman
recovering from bone cancer in
her right arm.

"A lot of kids would stay
home and sit on the couch and
moan, but not Stephanie," said
Monahan. "She's in here every
day."

Stephanie is still recovering
from chemotherapy treatments.
She wears a bandana on her
head and a cast on her arm. She
changes classes a few minutes
before other students to avoid
brittle bones getting jostled in
crowded hallways.

What's worse, Stephanie's brother, Kevin Hudon, an 18-year-old senior, was recently diagnosed with Hodgkin's lymphoma.

"I was just floored," said Monahan. "I couldn't believe this family had to go through this again. These are the nicest kids. She and her brother—you wouldn't even want them to have a bad day, let alone cancer."

The Hudons live with their aunt and two older cousins. When word got out that the family needed financial help, classmates began organizing a raffle.

When Monahan found out about Nathan Burditt's camping excursion outside Target, she made a joke about donating the PlayStation to the raffle.

Burditt surprised her by saying he'd think about donating. Shortly afterward, Monahan introduced him to Stephanie.

"I didn't say anything about her situation," said Monahan. "I just let him know who she was. He came back two classes later and said, 'You can have it.'"

Samantha Allard led the efforts to publicize the raffle and gather prizes. Allard was touched by Stephanie's spirit.

"Stephanie would come in even after her cancer treatments, and was always smiling," said Allard.

Jewelry, Manchester Monarchs game tickets, a Candy Kingdom gift basket, and more were raffled to raise money for the Hudons. And thanks to Nathan Burditt, one lucky winner walked away with a still-in-the-box PlayStation 3.

Burditt downplayed his philanthropy, saying he's not obsessed with gaming. He puts in 35 hours a week at Sam's Club making $8.40 an hour, and he said the money will eventually build back up.

"I've been through tough times," he said with a shrug. "I've seen what cancer can do to families."

What Burditt doesn't say is that he's already faced his own mortality, and the experience may have reshuffled his priorities. The 18-year-old had heart surgery this past summer.

"I think he had one of those moments where he questioned what's important in life," said Monahan.

Burditt's selfless donation left Stephanie beaming yesterday.

"I'm just glad that somebody actually thinks of other people," she said, "and I thank him a lot."[2]

Giving your time, a listening ear, a prayer, or even a PlayStation to someone else can result in a pretty good day—for you *and* that someone else. Before you know it, those pretty good days stack up to build pretty good years and a pretty good *life*.

An hour is too short, a year too long. Days are the bite-size portions of life, the God-designed segments of life management.

{ *Days are the bite-size portions of life.* }

Eighty-four thousand heartbeats.

One thousand four hundred forty minutes.

A complete rotation of the earth.

A circle of the sundial.

Two dozen flips of the hourglass.

Both a sunrise *and* a sunset.

A brand-spanking-new unsoiled, untouched, uncharted, and unused day!

A gift of twenty-four unlived, unexplored hours.

And if you can stack one good day on another and another, you will link together a good life.

But here's what you need to keep in mind.

You no longer have yesterday. It slipped away as you slept. It is gone. You can't change, alter, or improve it. Hourglass sand won't flow upward. The second hand of the clock refuses to tick backward. The monthly calendar reads left to right, not right to left. You no longer have yesterday.

You do not yet have tomorrow. Unless you accelerate the orbit of the earth or convince the sun to rise twice before it sets once, you can't live tomorrow today. You can't spend tomorrow's money, celebrate tomorrow's achievements, or resolve tomorrow's riddles. You have only today. This is the day the Lord has made.

Live in it. You must be present to win. Don't make today heavy with yesterday's regrets or acidize it with tomorrow's troubles. But don't we tend to do just that?

We do to our day what I did to a bike ride. My friend and I went on an extended hill-country trek. A few minutes into the trip I began to tire. Within a half hour my thighs ached and my lungs heaved like a beached whale. I could scarcely pump the pedals. I'm no Tour de France contender, but neither am I a newcomer, yet I felt like one. After forty-five minutes I had to dismount and catch my breath. That's when my partner spotted the problem. Both rear brakes were rubbing my back tire! Rubber grips contested every pedal stroke. The ride was destined to be a tough one.

Don't we do the same? Guilt presses on one side. Dread

drags the other. We sabotage our day, lugging along yesterday's troubles, downloading tomorrow's struggles. We aren't making today truly count.

How can we? What can we do? Here's my proposal: consult Jesus. The Ancient of Days has something to say about our days. He doesn't use the term *day* very often in Scripture. But the few times he does use it provide a delightful formula for upgrading each of ours to blue-ribbon status.

SATURATE YOUR DAY IN HIS GRACE.

"I tell you in solemn truth," replied Jesus, "that this very day you shall be with me in Paradise." (Luke 23:43 WEY)

ENTRUST YOUR DAY TO HIS OVERSIGHT.

"Give us day by day our daily bread." (Luke 11:3 NKJV)

ACCEPT HIS DIRECTION.

"If any of you want to be my followers, you must forget about yourself. You must take up your cross each day and follow me." (Luke 9:23 CEV)

Grace. Oversight. Direction.
G-O-D

Make this day count. Fill it with God. Give the day a chance. And while you're at it, keep an eye out for the seagull with the silly grin.

Remember GOD:
Grace. Oversight. Direction.

Daylifter

The next time you are stuck in a bad day, check your outlook with these three questions:

1. What do I feel guilty about?
2. What am I worried about?
3. What am I about?

Now, reflect on your answers with these reminders:

- Yesterday . . . forgiven.
- Tomorrow . . . surrendered.
- Today . . . clarified.

Jesus' design for a good day makes perfect sense. His grace erases guilt. His oversight removes fear. His direction removes confusion.

CHAPTER 2

Gratitude for Ungrateful Days

EXCERPTS FROM THE DIARY OF A DOG:

8:00 a.m.	Oh boy, dog food—my favorite!
9:30 a.m.	Oh boy, a car ride—my favorite!
9:40 a.m.	Oh boy, a walk—my favorite!
10:30 a.m.	Oh boy, another car ride—my favorite!
11:30 a.m.	Oh boy, more dog food—my favorite!
12:00 p.m.	Oh boy, the kids—my favorite!
1:00 p.m.	Oh boy, the yard—my favorite!
4:00 p.m.	Oh boy, the kids again—my favorite!
5:00 p.m.	Oh boy, dog food again—my favorite!
5:30 p.m.	Oh boy, Mom—my favorite!
6:00 p.m.	Oh boy, playing ball—my favorite!
8:30 p.m.	Oh boy, sleeping in my master's bed—my favorite!

EXCERPTS FROM THE DIARY OF A CAT:

Day 283 of my captivity. My captors continue to taunt me with bizarre little dangling objects. They dine lavishly on fresh meat, while I'm forced to eat dry cereal. I'm sustained by the hope of escape and the mild satisfaction I derive from ruining a few pieces of furniture. Tomorrow I may eat another houseplant. I attempted to kill my captors this morning by weaving through their walking feet. Nearly succeeded. Must try this strategy at the top of the stairs. Seeking to disgust and repulse these vile oppressors, I once again induced myself to vomit on their favorite chair. Must try this on their bed. To display my diabolical disposition, I decapitated a mouse and deposited the headless body on their kitchen floor. They only cooed and condescended, patting my head and calling me a "strong little kitty." Hmm—not working according to plan. During a gathering of their accomplices, they placed me in solitary confinement. I overheard that my confinement was due to my power of allergies. Must learn what this means and how to use it to my advantage.

I am convinced the other household captives are flunkies, perhaps snitches. The dog is routinely released and seems naively happy to return. He is, no doubt, a half-wit. The bird speaks with the humans regularly. Must be an informant. I am certain he reports my every move. Due to his current placement in the metal cage, his safety is assured, but I can wait. It is only a matter of time.[1]

The day of a dog. The day of a cat. One content, the other conniving. One at peace, the other at war. One grateful, the other grumpy. Same house. Same circumstances. Same master. Yet two entirely different attitudes.

Which diary reads more like yours? If your private thoughts were made public, how often would the phrase "Oh boy, my favorite" appear?

- "Oh boy, sunup—my favorite!"
- "Oh boy, breakfast—my favorite!"
- "Oh boy, homework—my favorite!"
- "Oh boy, chores—my favorite!"
- "Oh boy, a trip to the dentist—my favorite!"

Well, not even a dog would relish a trip to the dentist. But wouldn't we like to relish more of our day? We can. Begin with God's grace. As we accept his forgiveness, our day of gripes and groans becomes a day of gratitude.

{ *Begin with God's grace.* }

Matthew's day was lifted because of gratitude—not because of his own gratitude, but because someone else chose gratitude over a grudge.

have a cousin, Stephen, in my same grade at school. He's much cooler than me—always has friends hanging around him and a girlfriend to sit beside at lunch. Last week, when we were sitting in English class, Stephen pulled out a can of [chewing] tobacco. The whole back of the class saw him; then they turned and looked at me. *Great*, I thought. *What am I supposed to do? Keep my mouth shut? Act like it's cool?*

"Put that up," I whispered. "If you get caught, you'll get kicked out of school!"

He frowned and rolled his eyes at me. I'd seen that look before, and it said one thing: "Dork."

After class, some of those who saw him surrounded me. "You need to turn him in," they pressured. I didn't know what to do. I knew if I turned him in at school, he'd probably get expelled. Still, I knew if I didn't tell, someone else would, and he'd get in trouble anyway.

That afternoon, I told my dad, since my dad and Stephen's dad are brothers. My dad's not a man of many words. "I'll take care of it," he said. And I knew he would.

My mom sensed I was freaked out. She reassured me, saying I had done the Christian thing by addressing it with Stephen first and then taking the next step. But I knew Stephen wouldn't see it that way. "Christian thing" or not, he was going to get in trouble, and tomorrow I would have to face him again at school.

I played it over in my mind. *Maybe he'll never speak to me again, the cousin who ratted him out. Or maybe he and his cool friends will sit in the back of the class, sneering names like "snitch" and "rat." Or even better, maybe he'll just walk up to me and punch me in front of everyone.*

The next day at school, he walked up to me. I cringed. He

smiled, put his arm around me, and said, "Thanks for saying something before I got caught at school. You probably kept me from getting kicked out. You're the best cousin a guy could have." I was floored. I just knew he would hate me, but instead he chose to look at the good that came out of it.

Matthew, age 13

Yes, gratitude can turn a day, a friendship, or a family tie around completely. Gratitude is born from grace. It's the way of the forgiven. It is so appropriate, in fact, that its absence surprises Jesus. We know this because of ten men he healed.

> It happened that as he made his way toward Jerusalem, he crossed over the border between Samaria and Galilee. As he entered a village, ten men, all lepers, met him. They kept their distance but raised their voices, calling out, "Jesus, Master, have mercy on us!" (Luke 17:11–13)

Lepers. A huddle of half-draped faces and bent bodies. Who could tell where one form stopped and the other began as they leaned against one another? But who else could they lean on?

Their appearance repulsed people: lumps on the cheeks, nose, lips, and forehead. Ulcerated vocal cords rendered their voices a raspy wheeze. Hairless eyebrows turned eyes into hollow stares. Muscles and tendons contracted until hands looked like claws. People avoided lepers.

But Christ had compassion on them. So when people stepped back from the ten lepers, the Master stepped forward. "'Go, show yourselves to the priests.' They went, and while still on their way, became clean" (17:14).

Wouldn't you have loved to witness the miracle? No therapy. No treatment. No medicine. Just one prayer to one man and POW! Complete healing. Gnarled hands straightening. Open sores closing. Energy pulsating through veins. Ten hoods thrown back and twenty crutches dropped. A mass of misery becomes a leaping, jumping celebration of health.

Can you imagine how the lepers felt? If you're in Christ, you can. What he did for the lepers physically, he has done for you spiritually.

Sin makes lepers of us all, turns us into spiritual corpses. To the Ephesian Christians, Paul wrote, "In the past your spiritual lives were dead because of your sins and the things you did wrong against God" (Ephesians 2:1 ICB). The thoughts of the unbeliever, Paul argued, "are worth nothing. . . . They know nothing, because they refuse to listen. So they cannot have the life that God gives" (4:17–18 ICB).

Could it sound any gloomier?
Dead in sin.
Worthless in thought.
Darkened in understanding.
Separated from God.

Coroners give brighter reports. But Paul wasn't finished. Apart from Christ we are "without hope and without

God" (Ephesians 2:12 NIV), "controlled by the sinful nature" (Romans 7:5 NIV), and slaves of Satan (2 Timothy 2:26). What Jesus saw in the lepers' bodies, he sees in the sinner's soul—utter devastation. But what he did for them, he does for the willing heart. "Because of his great love for us, God, who is rich in mercy, made us alive with Christ even when we were dead in transgressions" (Ephesians 2:4–5 NIV).

He closes the open sores of our heart and straightens the gnarled limbs of our inner being. He swaps sin rags for righteous robes. He still heals. And he still looks for gratitude.

> When one of them saw that he was healed, he went back to Jesus, praising God in a loud voice. Then he bowed down at Jesus' feet and thanked him. (And this man was a Samaritan.) Jesus said, "Weren't ten men healed? Where are the other nine? Is this Samaritan the only one who came back to thank God?" (Luke 17:15–18 NCV)

The returning leper caught the attention of Christ. So did the absence of the others. Don't miss the headline of this story: God notices the grateful heart. Why? Does he have an ego problem? No. But we do. Gratitude lifts our eyes off the things we lack so we might see the blessings we possess. Nothing blows the winter out of the day like the Caribbean breeze of thankfulness.

{ God notices the grateful heart. }

Major in the grace of God. When Paul sent Timothy off to spiritual university, he told him to major in the grace of God: "You therefore, my son, *be strong in the grace* that is in Christ Jesus" (2 Timothy 2:1 NKJV).

Do the same. Focus on the cross. It's so easy to be distracted—so easy to be ungrateful, to make the mistake of Scott Simpson's caddy.

Scott is a professional golfer who plays often at the Masters Golf Tournament, hosted by the Augusta National Golf Club. Augusta National is to golfers what the Smithsonian is to history buffs: the ultimate experience. The course explodes in beauty. You would think you'd walked into an oil painting. Groomers manicure the course as if she's a wedding-day bride. In describing the perfection to his caddy, Scott commented, "You won't see a single weed all week."

Imagine Scott's surprise when, on Sunday, after five days of walking the course, his caddy pointed to the ground and announced to Scott, "I found one!"

Don't we do the same? We dwell in a garden of grace. God's love sprouts around us like lilacs and towers over us like Georgia pines. But we go on weed hunts. How many flowers do we miss in the process?

If you look long enough and hard enough, you'll find something to bellyache about. So quit looking! The caddy missed the good, the beauty of the course, because he was too busy looking for the bad, the weeds. Stop weed hunting! Look around for the flowers, and major in the grace of God.

Measure the gifts of God. Collect your blessings. Catalog

his kindnesses. List your reasons for gratitude, and recite them. "Always be joyful. Pray continually, and give thanks whatever happens. That is what God wants for you in Christ Jesus" (1 Thessalonians 5:16–18 NCV).

{ Measure the gifts of God. }

Look at the totality of those terms. *Always* be joyful. Pray *continually*. Give thanks *whatever* happens. Learn a lesson from Sidney Connell. When her brand-new bicycle was stolen, she called her dad with the bad news. He expected his daughter to be upset. But Sidney wasn't crying. She was honored. "Dad," she boasted, "out of all the bikes they could have taken, they took mine."

Gratitude is always an option. Matthew Henry made it his. When the famous scholar was accosted by thieves and robbed, he wrote this in his diary: "Let me be thankful first, because I was never robbed before; second, because, although they took my purse, they did not take my life; third, although they took my all, it was not much; and, fourthly, because it was I who was robbed, not I who robbed."[2]

Need spice in your day? Thank God for every problem that comes down the pike. Is any situation so horrible that gratitude is impossible? Some of the ladies at the Women of Faith Conference thought it was. The president, Mary Graham, told me about one particular weekend in which a shortage of space tested everyone's patience.

The floor had 150 fewer seats than needed. The arena staff tried to solve the problem by using narrow chairs. As a result, everyone had a place to sit, but they were crowded. Complaints filled the air like a bad perfume. Mary asked Joni Eareckson Tada, a speaker for the evening, if she could calm the crowd. Joni was perfectly qualified to do so. A childhood diving accident has left her wheelchair-bound. The attendants rolled her onto the platform, and Joni addressed the unhappy crowd. "I understand some of you don't like the chair in which you are sitting. Neither do I. But I have about a thousand handicapped friends who would gladly trade places with you in an instant."

The grumbling ceased.

Yours can too. Major in the grace of God. Measure the gifts of God. Who knows what you might record in your journal:

- "Mondays, oh boy—my favorite!"
- "Test days, oh boy—my favorite!"
- "Report-card day, oh boy—my favorite!"

Impossible, you say? How do you know? How do you know until you give every day a chance?

Be careful what you think, because your thoughts run your life.
Proverbs 4:23 NCV

Daylifter

Two types of voices command your attention today. Negative ones fill your mind with doubt, bitterness, and fear. Positive ones give hope and strength. Which ones will you choose to listen to? You have a choice, you know. "We take every thought captive so that it is obedient to Christ" (2 Corinthians 10:5 GOD'S WORD).

Do you let anyone who knocks on your door enter your house? Of course not. So don't let every thought that surfaces dwell in your mind. Take it captive . . . make it obey Jesus. If it doesn't, don't think it.

Negative thoughts never strengthen you. How many times have you cleared up a pimple with your grumbles? Does groaning about failing grades make them disappear? Why moan about your aches and pains, problems and tasks?

Instead, embrace the gift of gratitude, and watch as God turns your days into something worth talking about.

CHAPTER 3

Forgiveness for Sour Days

Don't you just love cleaning your room? Yeah. Not so much. But it's unavoidable. You know that when the clothes overflow into the hallway and an unidentifiable odor seeps into the rest of the house, you're going to get that look from your mom—the one you don't even think about talking back to. Then you know: it's time to clean your room.

The next hours—or days, if you've reached the ultimate level of pigdom—are spent sifting through stinky socks, paper wads, candy wrappers, computer and phone cables, photos of old girlfriends decorated with mustaches, and, *ewww*, is that a glass of soured milk?! And then, when you think you can't possibly lift another finger, it's done. You look around. You have a bed, a dresser, *and* space to walk between the bed and the dresser. Now, admit it, doesn't that feel good? (It's okay. Just admit it in your head; your mom will never know.)

When we let the clutter pile up around us, chaos and dread are the only real results. And when we make the effort, however forced, to clear the clutter, peace and optimism replace that chaos and dread.

But we all do it, don't we? We all let the clutter pile up until it threatens to swallow us completely. Not only in our houses or bedrooms, but in our hearts. Not the junk of papers and boxes, but the leftovers of anger and hurt. Do you pack-rat pain? Pile up offenses? Keep a record of slights? Do you let the unresolved conflicts of the past sit and turn sour in your mind and heart?

A tour of your heart might be telling. A pile of rejections stockpiled in one corner. Old insults filling another. Images of unkind people lining the wall, littering the floor.

No one can blame you. Innocence takers, promise breakers, wound makers—you've had your share. Yet doesn't it make sense to get rid of their trash? Want to make each day really count? Jesus says: *Give the grace you've been given.*

{ *Give the grace you've been given.* }

Take a long look at his reply to Peter's question: "'Lord, how often should I forgive someone who sins against me? Seven times?' 'No, not seven times,' Jesus replied, 'but seventy times seven!'" (Matthew 18:21–22 NLT).

That noise you hear is the sound of clicking calculators.

Seventy times seven equals 490 offenses, we discover. *Wow, I can get rid of my brother! He blew past this number a long time ago.*

But hang on. Before you write off your brother, you should probably sit in on this two-act play presented by Jesus himself:

ACT 1: GOD FORGIVES THE UNFORGIVABLE.

"The Kingdom of Heaven can be compared to a king who decided to bring his accounts up to date with servants who had borrowed money from him. In the process, one of his debtors was brought in who owed him millions of dollars. He couldn't pay, so his master ordered that he be sold—along with his wife, his children, and everything he owned—to pay the debt." (Matthew 18:23–25 NLT)

Such an immense debt. More literal translations say the servant owed 10,000 talents. One talent equaled 6,000 denarii. One denarius equaled one day's wage (Matthew 20:2). One talent, then, would equate to 6,000 days' worth of work. Ten thousand talents would represent 60 million days or 164,000 years of labor. A person earning $100 a day would owe $6 billion.

Whoa! What an astronomical sum. Jesus is just exaggerating to make a point, right? Or is he? One person would never owe such an amount to another. But might Jesus be referring to the debt we owe to God?

Let's calculate our indebtedness to him. How often do you sin in, say, an hour? To sin is to "fall short" (Romans 3:23 NIV). Worry is falling short on faith. Impatience is falling short on kindness. Being critical is falling short on love. How often do you come up short with God? For the sake of discussion, let's say ten times an hour and tally the results. Ten sins an hour, times sixteen waking hours (assuming we don't sin in our sleep), times 365, times the average male life span of seventy-five years. I'm rounding the total off at 4,380,000 sins per person.

Tell me, how do you plan to pay God for your 4.3 million sin increments? Your payout is unachievable. Unreachable. You're swimming in a Pacific Ocean of debt. Jesus' point precisely. The debtor in the story? You and me. The king? God. Look at what God does.

> "He [the servant] couldn't pay, so his master ordered that he be sold—along with his wife, his children, and everything he owned—to pay the debt. But the man fell down before his master and begged him, 'Please, be patient with me, and I will pay it all.' Then his master was filled with pity for him, and he released him and forgave his debt." (Matthew 18:25–27 NLT)

God pardons the zillion sins of selfish humanity. Forgives 60 million sin-filled days. "Out of sheer generosity he put us in right standing with himself. A pure gift. He got us out of the mess we're in and restored us to where he always wanted us to be. And he did it by means of Jesus Christ" (Romans 3:24).

God forgives the unforgivable. If this were the only point of the story, we'd have plenty to ponder. But this is only act 1 of the two-act play. The punch line is yet to come.

ACT 2: WE DO THE UNTHINKABLE.

The forgiven refuse to forgive.

> "But when the man left the king, he went to a fellow servant who owed him a few thousand dollars. He grabbed him by the throat and demanded instant payment. His fellow servant fell down before him and begged for a little more time. 'Be patient with me, and I will pay it,' he pleaded. But his creditor wouldn't wait. He had the man arrested and put in prison until the debt could be paid in full." (Matthew 18:28–30 NLT)

Unbelievable behavior! Multimillion-dollar forgiveness should produce a multimillion-dollar forgiver, shouldn't it? The hugely forgiven servant can himself forgive a small debt, can't he? This one doesn't. Note that he won't even wait (v. 30). He refuses to forgive. He could have. He should have. The forgiven should forgive. Which makes us wonder, did this servant truly accept the king's forgiveness? Did you notice what's missing from this story? Yep, gratitude. Notably absent from the parable is the joy of the forgiven servant. Like the nine ungrateful lepers we read about in the last chapter, this man never tells the king, "Thank you." He offers no words of appreciation, sings no song of celebration. His life has been spared, family freed, sentence lifted, Titanic-size debt forgiven—and he says zilch, nada, nothing. He should be hosting a Thanksgiving Day parade. He begs for mercy like a student on the brink of flunking out of college. But once he receives it, he acts as if he never scored less than a B.

Could his silence make the loudest point of the parable? "He who is forgiven little, loves little" (Luke 7:47 RSV). Apparently this man loves little because he had received little grace.

You know who I think this guy is? A grace rejecter.

He never accepts the grace of the king. He leaves the throne room with a sly smirk, as one who dodged a bullet, found a loophole, worked the system, pulled a fast one. He talked his way out of a jam. He chalks it up to his smooth talking rather than the grace of another. He bears the mark of the unforgiven: he refuses to forgive.

When the king hears about the servant's stingy heart, he blows his crown. He goes berserk:

"'You wicked servant! I forgave you all that debt because you begged me. Should you not also have had compassion on your fellow servant, just as I had pity on you?' And his master was angry, and delivered him to the torturers until he should pay all that was due to him. So My heavenly Father also will do to you if each of you, from his heart, does not forgive his brother his trespasses." (Matthew 18:32–35 NKJV)

The curtain falls on act 2, and we are left to ponder the

principles of the story. The big one comes quickly: *the grace-given give grace.* (Say *that* three times fast.) Forgiven people forgive people. The mercy-marinated drip mercy. "God is kind to you so you will change your hearts and lives" (Romans 2:4 NCV).

Sophomore Kyle McClure found himself facing some much-needed changes in his heart and life. But he soon discovered that God's grace and the support of Christian friends were enough to pull him back to the winning team.

CAMPUS LIFE

I Was Being a Hypocrite

By Kyle McClure, as told to Chris Lutes

My gym shoes squeaked on the wood floor as I went to block my opponent's shot. With my hands raised in front of his face, I pressed as close as I could without drawing a foul. Then I started the trash talk, saying whatever I could to put him down.

The coach had warned us against trash talk. "It's wrong!" he'd lectured us sternly. "It's just poor sportsmanship. Don't let me catch you doing it!"

As a Christian, I knew deep down inside he was right. Even so, I felt I had to do whatever it took to win. I couldn't let my team down.

I hadn't always felt that way. When I'd joined the team my freshman year, I'd wanted to live out the Christian beliefs I'd committed myself to in seventh grade. I did okay for a while. I read my Bible, prayed, and attended church and youth group. By my sophomore year, I was a student leader in my youth group.

31

Then I'd get together with the guys on the team, and I'd find myself slipping into their bad habits. Along with talking trash and acting pretty full of myself, I also let them influence the way I thought about other stuff. They'd pull out a *Playboy*, and I'd end up looking over their shoulders. They'd tell a dirty joke, and I'd find myself listening and laughing. Although I wouldn't go all the way, I'd often go further with girls than I knew was right.

I knew I was being a big hypocrite. But it was so hard to change. I felt like I was caught between two worlds.

I needed to make some serious changes. I started playing on a volleyball team with one of my best Christian friends. I asked him to hold me accountable for the way I lived my Christian life. We've set boundaries for ourselves that will help keep us from making mistakes we'd later regret.

I know I'm not perfect. Far from it. But I know when I mess up, God is always there to forgive me and help me do better the next time. In spite of my shortcomings, he is working in my life and helping me become more like the person he wants me to be.[1]

God's grace not only helped Kyle move past a difficult Christian struggle, but it also gave him hope in the ability to learn from his mistakes in the future. And with Kyle's grateful heart, you can be sure that the life-changing grace he experienced will overflow from him into a forgiving spirit for others.

Apple trees bear apples, wheat stalks produce wheat, and forgiven people forgive people. Grace is the natural outgrowth of grace.

The forgiven who won't forgive can expect a sad fate—a life full of many bad and bitter days. The "master . . . delivered him to the torturers until he should pay all that was due to him" (Matthew 18:34 NKJV).

You can take this route, or you can clean up your room, clean out your heart, and make this day count!

"But, Max, the hurt is so deep."

I know. The people who hurt you took much. But why let them keep taking from you? Haven't they stolen enough? Refusing to forgive keeps them there, hanging around, still taking.

"But, Max, what they did was so bad."

You bet it was. Forgiveness does not mean approval. You aren't supporting misbehavior. You are handing your offender over to "Him who judges righteously" (1 Peter 2:23 NKJV).

"But, Max, I've been so angry for so long."

And forgiveness won't come overnight. But you can take baby steps in the direction of grace. Forgive in phases. Quit hating the offender. Start praying for him. Try to understand her situation.

{ Forgiveness won't come overnight. }

Let Antwone Fisher inspire you. He had ample reason to live with a cluttered heart. For the first thirty-three years of his life, he knew neither of his parents. His father had died before Antwone was born. And his mother, for reasons he longed to know, abandoned him as a boy. He grew up as a foster child in Cleveland, abused, neglected, and desperate to find a single member of his family.

Equipped with the name of his father and a Cleveland phone book, he began calling people of the same last name. His life changed the day an aunt answered the phone. He told her his date of birth and his father's identity. He described the difficult turns his life had taken: being kicked out by his foster mom, serving a stint in the navy, now working as a security guard in Los Angeles.

Her voice was warm. "You have a big family." Before long, another aunt invited him to Cleveland for a Thanksgiving reunion and filled the week with a lifetime of belated love.

And then, after days of calls and attempts, his family found his mother's brother. He offered to take Antwone to the housing project where she lived. On the drive Antwone rehearsed the questions he'd longed to ask for the last three decades:

Why didn't you come for me?

Didn't you ever wonder about me?

Didn't you miss me at all?

But the questions were never uttered. The door opened, and Antwone walked into a dimly lit apartment with shabby furniture. Turning, he saw a frail woman who looked too old to be his mother. Her hair was uncombed. She wore her nightclothes.

Antwone's uncle said to her, "This is Antwone Quenton Fisher." Antwone's mother made the connection and started to moan, losing her footing, holding on to a chair. "Oh, God, please . . . oh, God." She turned her face away in shame and hurried out of the room crying.

Antwone learned that his mother had tried to get a man to marry her so she could raise her son but couldn't. She had gone on to bear four other children, also raised as wards of the state. Over the years she'd been hospitalized, incarcerated, and put on probation. When he realized how painful her years had been, he chose to forgive.

He writes, "Though my road had been long and hard, I finally understood that my mother's had been longer and harder. . . . Where the hurt of abandonment had lived inside me, now there was only compassion."[2]

In the end, we all choose what lives inside us.

May you choose forgiveness.

God's desire, his plan, his ultimate goal is to make you into the image of Christ.

Daylifter

ere's God's plan for your day: to make you more like Jesus.

"God . . . decided from the outset to shape the lives of those who love him along the same lines as the life of his Son" (Romans 8:29). Do you see what God is doing? Shaping you "along the same lines as the life of his Son."

Jesus felt no guilt; God wants you to feel no guilt.

Jesus had no bad habits; God wants to do away with yours.

Jesus faced fears with courage; God wants you to do the same.

Jesus knew the difference between right and wrong; God wants us to know the same.

Jesus served others and gave his life for the lost; we can do likewise.

How can you be more like Jesus today?

CHAPTER 4

Peace for Stressed-Out Days

Let's make a list. The advantages of stress.

Here's the first entry: *stress helps our health*. Lose sleep and live longer. A nervous stomach is a happy stomach, isn't it? Actually, no. Worry has been cited for a swarm of sicknesses: heart trouble, high blood pressure, rheumatism, ulcers, colds, thyroid malfunction, arthritis, migraine headaches, blindness, and a host of stomach disorders.[1] Hmm. Worry, it seems, hurts our health. But at least worry makes us feel better.

Worry brings joy. Worry puts the blue in the sky, the spring in the step, and the song in the bird. A dose of anxiety spices up the day, right? For that reason, we plan "worry vacations." Others camp, fish, shop, or hit the beach. You and I plan seven days of worry.

- Monday: stress out over that English test.
- Tuesday: dread tonight's homework.
- Wednesday: enumerate all the types of germs floating in the air.
- Thursday: list the reasons you'll never make it to college.
- Friday: calculate the number of injuries that can occur on a soccer field.
- Saturday: envision life without a parent.
- Sunday: record all the characteristics people don't like in us.

Worry is to joy what a vacuum cleaner is to dirt: might as well attach your heart to a happiness-sucker and flip the switch.

Let's keep thinking. Surely anxiety has some value. Even if it takes health and steals joy, doesn't worry usher in some blessing? How about this one? *Worry solves our problems.* Treat your troubles to a good dose of fret and watch them disappear. Correct?

Wrong again. Does dreading tomorrow's homework ever get it done? Nope. Anxiety doesn't end the problems. Let's just face it. Anxiety has no advantages at all. It ruins health, robs joy, and changes nothing.

Katie Redner's anxiety was about her appearance. She was so worried about how others saw her and how she saw herself that she had overlooked the most important viewpoint of all: God's.

was seventeen years old and consumed by the desire to be considered "beautiful." It was a trap, and I needed help. I finally admitted I had been struggling with an eating disorder for four years. Two months later, I found myself in Ridgeview Institute, twenty pounds underweight, eating less than five hundred calories a day, and exercising a minimum of three hours a day. But when I looked in the mirror, I still saw something hideous. For two months, I worked hard in the hospital until I was strong enough to return to a somewhat normal life.

I came out of Ridgeview with meal plans, a few gained pounds, and new "coping skills" to deal with life as I saw it. But nothing could have prepared me for what was next. After being out of treatment for one month, I was given the opportunity to participate in World Vision's 30-Hour Famine. I was torn. It was a great event with a great cause, but I found myself asking some hard questions. How could I support the battle against world hunger when I myself denied the gift of food? I signed up for the event anyway. And in the end I realized that I should use my story as a reason, not an excuse.

After the event our group was presented with the chance to be a part of World Vision's Study Tour program that allows students and leaders to see firsthand where the program's money was going. Before I knew it, I was on a plane heading for Uganda, Africa. I could not figure out why God had chosen me for this trip, but he had something in store that changed my life forever.

For the first part of the trip we were in Gulu, Uganda, where they struggled with feeding refugees from civil war. We were able to visit a food distribution center, and I was immediately thrown into a small tent filled with young women and children. The children were malnourished, and they were in the tent to be weighed and have their progress checked. The mothers, desperate for food, would thrust their tiny, crying children into my arms. As I held them, my heart shattered into a million pieces. They deserved more. Why was this happening to them? But when I looked into their eyes, I saw Christ looking back at me. It was there, in the middle of chaos and with the most beautiful children I have ever seen, that I finally understood. Just like that hungry baby, I was a child of God. I deserved more too. I was beautiful too.

As I left, I took away a brand-new outlook on life. For so long I had been starving—both physically and spiritually. God's comfort and light had always been there, all I had to do was reach out and take it. I now live every day knowing that God knows I'm beautiful, and he's holding my hand.[2]

Katie

Katie's physical and spiritual health had deteriorated because of her anxiety. And it was only when she started to break through her anxiety that she began to see the plan God had in store for her. Don't allow your worries to obstruct the view of God's plan for you.

To guide us, Christ offers a worry-bazooka. Remember how he taught us to pray? "Give us day by day our daily bread" (Luke 11:3 NKJV).

This simple sentence unveils God's provision plan: *live one day at a time.* God disclosed the strategy to Moses and the Israelites in the wilderness. Heaven knew they needed it. The freed slaves had taken anxiety to a new art form. You'd think they would have given seminars on faith.

They had witnessed the plagues, walked on dry ground through the Red Sea, and watched the Egyptian soldiers drown. They had beheld one miracle after another, but still they worried:

The whole community of Israel complained about Moses and Aaron. "'If only the LORD had killed us back in Egypt,' they moaned. 'There we sat around pots filled with meat and ate all the bread we wanted. But now you have brought us into this wilderness to starve us all to death'" (Exodus 16:2–3 NLT).

Wait a minute. Are these the same people the Egyptians beat and overworked? The same Hebrews who cried to God for deliverance? And now, just a month into freedom, they speak as if Egypt were a paid vacation. They've forgotten. They've forgotten the miracles they saw and the misery they knew.

Forgetfulness begets fretfulness.

But God, patient as he is with memory loss, sends reminders.

Then the LORD said to Moses, "Look, I'm going to rain down food from heaven for you. Each day the people can go out and pick up as much food as they need for that day. I will test them in this to see whether or not they will follow my instructions. On the sixth day they will gather food, and when they prepare it, there will be twice as much as usual." (vv. 4–5 NLT)

Note the details of God's plan to provide.

He meets daily needs daily. Quail covered the compound

in the evenings; manna glistened like fine frost in the mornings. Meat for dinner. Bread for breakfast. The food fell every day. Not annually, monthly, or hourly, but daily. And there is more.

{ *He meets daily needs daily.* }

He meets daily needs miraculously. When the people first saw the wafers on the ground, "the Israelites took one look and said to one another, *man-hu* (What is it?). They had no idea what it was" (v. 15).

The stunned people named the wafers *man-hu*, Hebrew for "What in the world is this?" God had resources they knew nothing about, solutions beyond their reality, provisions outside their possibility. They saw the scorched earth; God saw heaven's bread basket. They saw dry land; God saw a covey of quail behind every bush. They saw problems; God saw provision.

Anxiety fades as our memory of God's goodness doesn't.

When my daughters were single-digit ages—two, five, and seven—I wowed them with a miracle. I told them the story of Moses and the manna and invited them to follow me on a wilderness trek through the house.

"Who knows?" I suggested. "Manna may fall from the sky again."

We dressed in sheets and sandals and did our best Bedouin hike through the bedrooms. The girls, on my instruction, complained to me, Moses, of hunger and demanded I take them back to Egypt, or at least to the kitchen. When we entered the den, I urged them to play up their parts: groan, moan, and beg for food.

"Look up," I urged. "Manna might fall at any minute."

Two-year-old Sara obliged with no questions, but Jenna and Andrea had their doubts. How can manna fall from a ceiling?

Just like the Hebrews. "How can God feed us in the wilderness?"

Just like you? You look at tomorrow's demands, next week's assignments, next month's silent calendar. Your future looks as barren as the Sinai Desert. "How can I face my future?" God tells you what I told my daughters: "Look up."

When my daughters did, manna fell! Well, not manna, but vanilla wafers dropped from the ceiling and landed on the carpet. Sara squealed with delight and started munching. Jenna and Andrea were old enough to request an explanation.

My answer was simple. I knew the itinerary. I knew we would enter this room. Vanilla wafers fit safely on the topside of the ceiling-fan blades. I had placed them there in advance. When they groaned and moaned, I turned on the switch.

God's answer to the Hebrews was similar. Did he know their itinerary? Did he know they would grow hungry? Yes and yes. And at the right time, he tilted the manna basket toward earth.

And what about you? God knows what you need and where you'll be. Any chance he has some vanilla wafers on tomorrow's ceiling fans? Trust him. "Give your entire attention to what God is doing right now, and don't get worked up about what may or may not happen tomorrow. God will help you deal with whatever hard things come up when the time comes" (Matthew 6:34).

The Greek word for worry, *merimnao*, stems from the verb *merizo* (divide) and the noun *nous* (mind). Worry slashes the mind, splitting thoughts between today and tomorrow. Today stands no chance against it. Fretting over tomorrow's problems today siphons the strength you need for now, leaving you weak.

Worry gives small problems big shadows. Montaigne said, "My life has been full of terrible misfortunes, most of which never happened."[3] Corrie ten Boom commented, "Worry does not empty tomorrow of its sorrows; it empties today of its strength."[4] Worry scuttles our lives, hurts us, and most sadly, dishonors God.

God's Word says, "Every detail in our lives of love for God is worked into something good" (Romans 8:28).

Worry takes a look at catastrophes and groans, "It's all coming unraveled."

God's Word says, "[God has] done it all and done it well" (Mark 7:37).

Worry disagrees: "The world has gone crazy."

God's Word calls God "the blessed controller of all things" (1 Timothy 6:15 PHILLIPS).

Worry wonders if anyone is in control.

God's Word declares, "God will take care of everything you need" (Philippians 4:19).

Worry whispers this lie: "God doesn't know what I need."

God's Word reasons, "Consider the ravens: They do not sow or reap, they have no storeroom or barn; yet God feeds them. And how much more valuable you are than birds!" (Luke 12:24 NIV).

Worry disagrees and replies, "You're on your own. It's you against the world."

Worry wages war on your faith. You know that. You hate to worry. But what can you do to stop it? These three worry stoppers deserve your consideration:

Pray more. No one can pray and worry at the same time. When we worry, we aren't praying. When we pray, we aren't worrying. "You will keep him in perfect peace, whose mind is stayed on You, because he trusts in You" (Isaiah 26:3 NKJV).

When you pray, you "stay" your mind on Christ, resulting in peace. Bow your knees and banish anxiety.

Want less. Most anxiety stems not from what we need but from what we want.

"Delight yourselves in God, yes, find your joy in him at all times" (Philippians 4:4 PHILLIPS). If God is enough for you, then you'll always have enough because you'll always have God.

Live for today. Heaven still has her manna house. The bushes still hide quail. And you still have today. Don't sacrifice it on the altar of anxiety. "Live only for the hour and its allotted work. . . . Set earnestly at the little task at your elbow . . . our plain duty is 'not to see what lies dimly at a distance, but to do what lies clearly at hand.'"[5]

May I urge you to do the same? "Go confidently to the throne of God's kindness to receive mercy and find kindness, which will help us at *the right time*" (Hebrews 4:16 GOD'S WORD).

Some of my friends saw an example of God's perfect timing during a trip to Natal, Brazil. They were conducting a children's seminar at a delightful congregation called Refugio da Graca. The church is situated five minutes from a tall bridge that has become infamous for suicide attempts. So many people have taken their lives by jumping from the structure that the church held a prayer vigil specifically for the bridge. Their prayers saw fruit when my friends were walking past at the very moment a woman was about to jump. She had climbed over the railing and was only a step from death. With much persuasion and effort, they talked her back from the ledge and saved her life.

Remarkably, their walk across the bridge was not in their original plan. They had been eating lunch at a restaurant and needed to return to the church building for the afternoon session. But the person scheduled to pick them up was late; hence, they chose to walk back. Their host was tardy, but God was right on time.

Isn't he always? He sends help at the hour we need it.

{ He sends help at the hour we need it. }

You don't have wisdom for tomorrow's problems. But you will tomorrow. You don't have resources for tomorrow's needs. But you will tomorrow. You don't have courage for tomorrow's challenges. But you will when tomorrow comes.

What you do have is manna for the morning and quail for the evening: bread and meat for the day. God meets daily needs daily and miraculously. He did then, he does still, and he will for you.

You last the long race by running short ones.

Daylifter

An accomplished Ironman triathlete told me the secret of his success. "You last the long race by running short ones." Don't swim 2.4 miles; just swim to the next buoy. Rather than bike 112 miles, ride 10, take a break, and bike 10 more. Never tackle more than the challenge ahead.

Didn't Jesus offer the same counsel? "So don't ever worry about tomorrow. After all, tomorrow will worry about itself. Each day has enough trouble of its own" (Matthew 6:34 GOD'S WORD).

You can't control your temper forever, but you can control it for the next hour. Earning a college degree can seem impossible, but studying one semester is manageable, and logging in one good week is doable.

Do you have a huge task looming? Does the thought of it sabotage your day? How can you break it down into manageable parts?

CHAPTER 5

Hope for Catastrophic Days

Vanderlei de Lima. He's just a whisper of a guy. At five feet five inches, he stands shorter than some seventh graders. But don't let the size of the little Brazilian fool you. The body may be small, but the heart is bigger than the Olympic Stadium in Athens. That's where he received the 2004 bronze medal for the marathon.

He should have won the gold. He was leading the race with only three miles to go when a spectator accosted him. A deranged protester from Ireland, who had been imprisoned for running on a Grand Prix racetrack in England a year earlier, hurled himself into the runner, forcing him off the course and into the crowd. Although stunned and shaken, de Lima collected himself and resumed the race. In the process he lost his rhythm, precious seconds, and his position.

But he never lost his joy. The small-bodied, big-hearted Brazilian entered the old marble stadium with the thrill of a child. He punched the air with his fists, then ran with both arms extended, like a human airplane looking for a place to land, weaving for joy.

Later, crowned with an olive wreath and bejeweled with an unflappable smile, he explained his exhilaration: "It is a festive moment. It is a unique moment. Most athletes never have this moment."

Yeah, but most athletes never get bumped off the path either.

Vanderlei de Lima never complained. "The Olympic spirit prevailed again. . . . I was able to medal for myself and my country."[1]

I'm taking notes on this guy. Wondering how de Lima kept such an attitude. Race bumpers still prowl the crowds. You don't have to run a marathon to go from the front of the pack to landing flat on your back. Just ask kids who gather at their mom's grave. Or patients waiting their turn for cancer therapy. Cemetery. Chemotherapy. The father who moved out, the soldier who returns missing a limb, the parents of the runaway daughter, the family made homeless by the hurricane.

Life catastrophically derailed. How do you get back in the race?

{ How do you get back in the race? }

Take Katie Pavlacka, for instance. Her parents noticed issues with her eyesight as early as age five, and by ninth grade, she was completely blind. She had quite a struggle coming to grips with her disability. It didn't help that kids were ruthless in teasing her. How would Katie ever get back in the race when she couldn't even see the track?

CAMPUS LIFE

Why Me?

By *Mark Moring*

Eighth grade. The jerks were everywhere.

Almost every time Katie Pavlacka turned a corner at school, they'd be waiting, ready to spring another dumb prank, for a few laughs at her expense.

Sometimes, they'd stick out a foot and trip her. Sometimes, they'd sneak up and slam her locker shut before she could grab what she'd come for. But their favorite stunt was the one with the sliding glass doors. They'd quietly close the doors as Katie approached, just to watch her walk—*wham!*—face first, smack into the glass.

"I kind of questioned, *Is there really a God and why is this happening to me?*" Katie, now 19, says today. "I was mad at God, and I took it out on a lot of people, especially my family.

"But I also kept a lot inside and beat myself up with all that anger. I was mad because I was different, and I didn't want to be different."

Then came the aide. That really sent Katie over the top. The school assigned a woman to help Katie with her tasks, but Katie didn't want any help. At all.

"She followed me to all my classes to help me take notes or whatever," says Katie. "But I felt like that was intruding into my freedom. I scared her away," Katie says with a laugh. "So they got me another aide—a younger, more lively one. I rebelled against her too, but she took a stand and took control. And by the time the school year ended, we went from being worst enemies to really good friends. She helped me accept my differences instead of fighting against them."

And then, in 9th grade, along came Michelle Weinberg.

"Michelle was always there, spending time with me, just being a friend," says Katie. "She invited me to her youth group activities. That's how I got serious about my faith again.

"It took me a couple of years before I came to realize that God *is* there and that he cares. I also came to realize that it was *my* faith now and not just something I had grown up with. I wanted to be serious about being a Christian and get to know God better."

Katie's had to learn a lot about being patient, about waiting on God and his perfect timing. *Patient* and *waiting*. They sound like such stagnant words, so motionless. But not for Katie. While she waited, she took a hard look at the challenges she faced and decided to dive right in. Literally.

She hit the water at first with a vengeance, to prove to others—and herself—that despite her failing eyesight, she would *still* excel at something. In time, that vengeance turned to passion and determination, so much that she swam more than three miles *before school* every day. She made the swim team her freshman year at Liverpool (NY) High School. And though she competed against sighted swimmers, she held her own.

Katie didn't stop there. She's now moved on to win titles in the Disability National Championships and a gold medal in the World Championships for the Blind in Madrid. In the meantime, Katie is a straight-A sophomore at Oneonta College in New York, where she's also on the swim team.

Katie "feels" her way through the water by brushing up against one of the lane ropes. And when it's time to make her turn, a coach touches her on the back with a tennis ball attached to the end of a pole. Or the spray from a sprinkler tells Katie she's near the end of her lane.

"I've also found that my blindness has helped me learn how important relationships are—to be able to talk to people and share my experiences. I've learned to communicate better with people and get to know them better. It's made my friendships deeper, I think.

"My blindness is just something that's happened to me," she says. "I just want to make the best of what I have and go from there."[2]

When her sight was gone, Katie felt her way down the track, quite literally. Let's turn to another athlete for a few more ideas. Take a look at him. Peer through the small window in the wall of the Roman jail. See the man in chains? The aging fellow with the stooped shoulders and hawkish nose? That's Paul, the imprisoned apostle. His chains never come off. The guards never leave. And he's probably wondering if he'll ever get out.

Bumped off track. Trouble had begun a couple years earlier in Jerusalem. Though Paul went out of his way to follow the Jewish laws, religious leaders accused him of blasphemy. They nearly killed him and then unfairly imprisoned him. They trashed his name, violated his rights, and disrupted his plans.

His Roman citizenship saved his neck. Entitled to a Roman hearing, he journeyed from Jerusalem to Rome. No Mediterranean cruise. Paul survived a hurricane, only to be bitten by a snake, and survived the snakebite, only to be stranded on an island for three months. When he was finally delivered to Rome, his case sat for *two years* in the Roman Empire.

By the time we find Paul in his cell, he has been beaten, lied about, storm tossed, rejected, and neglected.

Ah, but at least he has the church. At least he can take comfort in the thought of the very congregation he helped strengthen, right? Hardly. The Roman church is in trouble. From the jail cell, the apostle writes, "Some preach about Christ because they are jealous and ambitious. . . . [They] preach about Christ for selfish and wrong reasons, wanting to make trouble for me in prison" (Philippians 1:15, 17 NCV).

Power-hungry preachers occupy the pulpit. You expect such antics out of nonbelievers, but Christians preaching for personal gain? Paul is facing huge problems.

And who knows what Emperor Nero will do? He feeds disciples to the Colosseum lions for lunch. Does Paul have any guarantee that the same won't happen to him? His prison epistle word selection suggests he doesn't: "whether I live or die" (1:20 NCV). Then soon after: "Dying would be profit for me" (1:21 NCV). Paul is not naive. He knows that the only thing between him and death is a nod from moody Nero.

Paul has every reason to be stressed out.

Maybe you do too. Maybe you, like Paul, have been

bumped off track, held prisoner by the sum total of your bad breaks. And chained next to you is not a Roman guard but a diligent cohort of Satan, whose sole assignment is to stir the sour soup of self-pity. "Just look at all the bad things that have happened to you." He has a point. No one questions the fact of your misfortunes. But one would wisely question the wisdom of wallowing in them.

Paul doesn't. Out of all of the bad things that happened to him, he chooses to focus on the good. He itemizes not the mistreatments of people but the faithfulness of God.

"I want you to know, brethren" (Philippians 1:12 NKJV). This phrase is Paul's way of highlighting a paragraph. He uses similar wording elsewhere to headline his points.[3] In this case, it is important for the Philippians to know "that what has happened to me has really served to advance the gospel" (v. 12 NIV).

Have you ever lost your voice but not your health? You sound hoarse but still feel as healthy as one? People sympathize with your illness, only to hear you whisper, "I really feel fine. I know it sounds like I'm sick, but really . . ."

Paul is saying the same. He may appear to be bumped off track, but he is actually right on target. Why? One reason. Christ is preached. The mission is being accomplished. "It has become known throughout the whole praetorian guard and to all the rest that my imprisonment is for Christ" (v. 13 RSV).

The praetorian guard was a handpicked division of crack imperial troops. They received double pay and added benefits. They were the finest of the fine. And, in God's sovereignty, the finest of Caesar's soldiers are chained to the finest of God's. How much time passed before Paul realized what was happening? How long before Paul looked at the chains, looked at the bright West Point graduate jailer, and then smiled a smile toward heaven? *Hmm. Captive audience.* He leans toward the soldier. "Got a minute to talk?" or, "Would you mind proofreading this letter I'm writing?" or, "Can I tell you about a Jewish carpenter I know?"

His words meet their mark. Read this line from the Philippian benediction: "All of God's people greet you, particularly those from the palace of Caesar" (4:22 NCV).

The man may be shackled, but the message is not. The prison of Paul becomes the pulpit of Paul, and that is fine with him. Any method is fine as long as Christ is preached.

And any motive is fine as long as Christ is preached. Remember the problem with the preachers? Paul says they are "wanting to make trouble for me in prison" (Philippians 1:17 NCV). Does Paul dismiss the preachers because of their motives? No, he is thankful for them. "The important thing is that in every way, whether for right or wrong reasons, they are preaching about Christ" (v. 18 NCV).

Few passages in Scripture are punctuated with such faith. Paul displays absolute trust in God's oversight. So what if someone preaches from poor motives? Is God not greater than his people? He trumps bad preachers. The power is in the truth, not the instrument who delivers that truth.

Knowing this, Paul can write from the chill of the jail, "So I am happy, and I will continue to be happy" (v. 18 NCV).

Unfairly arrested. Unkindly treated. Uncharted future. Yet unbridled joy.

Bumped off track but still in the race. How? We can summarize all the reasons with one word. Reduce all the answers to a single verb. Distill the explanations into one decision. What is the word, the verb, the decision?

Trust.

{ *Trust.* }

Paul trusted the oversight of God. He didn't know why bad things happened. He didn't know how they would be resolved. But he knew who was in charge. And knowing who's in charge balances the mystery of why and how.

Over a hundred years ago in England, the borough of West Stanley endured a great tragedy. A mine collapsed, trapping and killing many of the workers inside. The bishop of Durham, Dr. Handley Moule, was asked to bring a word of comfort to the mourners. Standing at the mouth of the mine, he said, "It is very difficult for us to understand why God should let such an awful disaster happen, but we know Him and we trust Him, and all will be right. I have at home," he continued, "an old bookmark given to me by my mother. It is worked in silk, and, when I examine the wrong side of it, I see nothing but a tangle of threads, crossed and re-crossed. It looks like a big mistake. One would think that someone had done it who did not know what she was doing. But, when I turn it over and look at the right side, I see there, beautifully embroidered, the letters GOD IS LOVE.

"We are looking at this today," he counseled, "from the wrong side. Someday we shall see it from another standpoint, and shall understand."[4]

Indeed we shall. Until then, focus less on the tangled threads and more on the hand of the Weaver. Learn a lesson from Vanderlei de Lima: don't let the bumps in the race keep you from the award ceremony at its end.

> The next time you fight through stress, do the math. Does God consume 80 percent of your thoughts? He wants to.

Daylifter

Where is your mind on your tough days? During the Friday of the crucifixion, Jesus spoke thirteen times. Ten of those remarks were to or about God. Nearly 80 percent of his comments were about heaven. Jesus talked to or thought about God all day long.

When problems disturb you, take a break from them! "Don't shuffle along, eyes to the ground . . . Look up, and be alert to what is going on around Christ—that's where the action is" (Colossians 3:2).

Follow the resolve of Paul: "So we don't look at the troubles we can see now; rather, we fix our gaze on things that cannot be seen" (2 Corinthians 4:18 NLT).

Are you having a tough day? Turn it over to God.

CHAPTER 6

Fuel for Drained Days

If you ever see a guy walking on the side of the road carrying an empty gas can, remove your hat in respect. He's dying inside.

Girls see the empty gas tank as a mere inconvenience. Guys see it as the ultimate failure. Our first set of keys is handed to us with these words: "Make sure you buy some gas." From that moment on, the standard is set: take care of your machine.

All other measures of manhood pale in comparison. It matters not if you can transplant a heart or win a pentathlon. If you can't keep gas in your tank, you are of all men to be pitied. Even the toughest action hero weeps at the sound of that telltale *chug-sputter-cough*. Such moments are etched in the memory of the male mind.

They linger in mine. In the days before the Lucado girls had driver's licenses, I served as their morning chauffeur. We were pulling into the school parking lot one day when the car hiccupped. I looked down to see the gas needle resting on the wrong side of empty. Not wanting my daughters to see their father weep, I urged them to hurry on to class. It was one of my more noble gestures.

I then set about to solve the problem of the empty tank. I began by staring at the gauge, hoping it would move. Didn't work. Next I blamed my parents for potty training me too soon. Still no fuel. Denying the problem was my next approach. I put the car in gear and pressed the accelerator as if the tank were full. The car didn't budge.

Odd choices, you say? What do *you* do when you run out of gas? You don't exhaust your petroleum perhaps, but all of us run out of something. You need kindness, but the gauge is on empty. You need hope, but the needle is in the red. You want five gallons of solutions but can only muster a few drops. When you run out of steam before you run out of day, what do you do? Stare at the gauge? Blame your parents? Deny the problem?

No. Pity won't start the car. Complaints don't fuel an engine. Denial doesn't bump the needle. In the case of an empty tank, we've learned to get the car to a gas pump ASAP. In the case of the empty life or heart, however, we tend to make the mistake the disciples made.

They haven't run out of gas but out of food. Five thousand men and their families surround Jesus. They are getting hungry, and the disciples are getting antsy. "When it was late in the day, his followers came to him and said,

'No one lives in this place, and it is already very late'" (Mark 6:35 NCV).

His followers came to him. These five words imply that the followers had just left a meeting. A committee had been formed, convened, and dismissed, all in the absence of Jesus. The disciples didn't consult their leader; they just described the problems and then told him what to do.

Problem number one: location. "No one lives in this place."

Problem number two: time. "It is already very late."

Problem number three: budget. In a parallel passage, Philip, the deacon in charge of finance, produces a just-printed pie chart. "Someone would have to work almost a year to buy enough bread for each person to have only a little piece" (John 6:7 NCV).

Do you detect an attitude behind those phrases? "No one lives in this place." (Who picked this location?) "It is already very late." (Whoever preached forgot to watch the clock.) "Someone would have to work almost a year." (Why didn't these people bring their own food?) The disciples' frustration borders on downright irreverence. Rather than *ask* Jesus what to do, they *tell* Jesus what to do: "Send the people away so they can go to the country-side and towns around here to buy themselves something to eat" (Mark 6:36 NCV). The disciples tell Jesus to tell the people to get lost.

Not one of their finer moments. Shouldn't they have known better? This is not the first problem they've seen Jesus face or fix. Skip back through the scenes, and make a list of miracles they've witnessed. Water turned to wine, a boy healed in Capernaum, a boatload of fish caught at Galilee. They've seen Jesus raise a little girl from the dead, banish at least one demon, heal several paralytics and one mother-in-law. They've watched Jesus still a storm and resurrect a widow's son. So astounding were his healings that the following sentences appear in your Bible:

> Jesus healed many who had various diseases. He also drove out many demons. (Mark 1:34 NIV)

> Jesus went throughout Galilee . . . healing every disease and sickness among the people. . . . People brought to him all who were ill with various diseases, those suffering severe pain, the demon-possessed, those having seizures, and the paralyzed, and he healed them. (Matthew 4:23–24 NIV)

> The people all tried to touch him, because power was coming from him and healing them all. (Luke 6:19 NIV)

Veteran disciples have seen Jesus in action. The whole country has seen Jesus in action. He has earned a national reputation for doing the impossible. But do the disciples ask Jesus for his opinion? Does anyone in the committee meeting think about asking the miracle man what to do? Does John, Peter, or James raise a hand and say, "Hey, I've got an idea. Let's go talk to the one who stilled the storm and raised the dead. Maybe he has a suggestion"?

Please note: the mistake of the disciples was not that they calculated the problem but that they calculated without Christ. In giving Jesus no chance, they gave their day no chance. They reserved a table for twelve at the Restaurant of the Rotten Day.

How unnecessary! If your father were Steve Jobs and your computer broke, where would you turn? If Kate Spade were your mom and you needed a cute new purse, to whom would you go? If your father is God and you have a problem on your hands, what should you do?

> { If your father is God and you have a problem on your hands, what should you do? }

A couple thousand years later, our friend below does a little disciple reenactment. She knows God's power but doesn't trust in his plan. She, too, decides the solution and presents it to God. Wonder how he responds . . .

IGNITE YOUR FAITH

Didn't God Care?

By Amy Adair

"You're moving?" I asked, stunned. "Where?"

Tears fell down Andrea's cheeks. "To Texas," she said between deep sighs. "It's a thousand miles away."

I went home that night and couldn't stop crying. My best friend was moving, and I felt like God was totally letting me down. I had met Andrea right before my freshman year, and I always considered her friendship an answer to prayer. Before Andrea, I honestly didn't have one friend at school. I was the kid no one wanted to eat lunch with. For some reason, kids always teased me and made fun of me. I felt so alone.

I prayed every day that God would bring one person into my life who would be a friend. I'd almost given up hope, when my parents let me switch schools. That's when I met Andrea. We clicked instantly. She was a strong Christian and invited me to her youth group.

Now that Andrea was moving, I felt like God was taking back his answer to my prayer. I was sure I'd once again be the friendless girl who was lonely and depressed.

Andrea and I prayed that her family wouldn't have to leave. I was positive God would work some miracle so Andrea wouldn't have to go. But the day finally came when we had to say good-bye.

I started my junior year feeling more empty and alone than ever. One day, I ran into some of the kids from Andrea's youth group. I was surprised when they invited me to eat lunch with them. They encouraged me to come back to their youth group. I knew it wouldn't be the same without Andrea, but I agreed to go anyway.

I eventually told my youth pastor that I didn't understand why God hadn't answered my prayers. He explained that God answers all of my prayers, and with faith, I could have peace about God's answer, no matter what it was.

Then one night, while I was at youth group, it hit me that God had been listening to me. He had answered my prayers. Even though my best friend was no longer around, God had "replaced" her with an awesome youth group.

Although I still talk to Andrea on the phone and e-mail her all the time, I've grown really close to the kids from youth group. It didn't happen overnight, but I slowly started to open up to them. Not only have they all become my friends, but I can count on them to pray for me, too. I've even gained enough confidence to reach out and meet other people at school.

As hard as it was when Andrea moved, I can see God's hand in it all. If Andrea hadn't moved, I don't think I would have ever seen the need to make more friends in youth group. If Andrea was still going to my school, I probably wouldn't have gained the boldness and confidence I needed to reach out to others.

When I look back, I know God answered my prayers. I also know he had my best interests at heart.[1]

God responded to her the way he'll respond to us—if we'll just take our problems to him. He will provide solutions that are exponentially greater than any solution we could construct.

Scripture clearly defines the scope of God's solutions:

Is your problem too large? "God . . . is able . . . to accomplish infinitely more than we might ask or think" (Ephesians 3:20 NLT).

Is your need too great? "God is able to provide you with every blessing in abundance" (2 Corinthians 9:8 RSV).

Is your temptation too severe? "[He] is able to help us when we are being tested" (Hebrews 2:18 NLT).

Are your sins too numerous? "He is able, once and forever, to save those who come to God through him" (Hebrews 7:25 NLT).

Is your future too frightening? "God . . . is able to keep you from falling away and will bring you with great joy into his glorious presence without a single fault" (Jude v. 24 NLT).

Is your enemy too strong? "[God] is able even to subdue all things to Himself" (Philippians 3:21 NKJV).

Make these verses part of your daily diet. God is able to accomplish, provide, help, save, keep, subdue. . . . He is able to do what you can't. He already has a plan. Regarding the hungry crowd, "Jesus already knew what he planned to do" (John 6:6 NCV). God's not bewildered. Go to him.

Let's get practical. You and your sister are about to battle it out again. The thunderstorm looms on the horizon. The temperature is dropping, and lightning bolts are flashing. Both of you need patience, but both tanks are empty. What if one of you calls a time-out? What if one of you says, "Let's talk to Jesus before we talk to each other. In fact, let's talk to Jesus until we *can* talk to each other"? Couldn't hurt. After all, he calmed the stormy sea. Perhaps he could do the same for your relationship.

{ God is able to accomplish, provide, help, save, keep, subdue. }

Another example: your classmate is a complete slacker on a group project. You need ten buckets of patience yet have only a few drops. Rather than rush in and burn up what little patience you have, go first to Christ. Confess your weakness and ask for help. Who knows? He might take your few drops and multiply them into a few gallons.

That's what he did for a young boy. Look at how the story ends:

> Andrew . . . said, "There's a little boy here who has five barley loaves and two fish. But that's a drop in the bucket for a crowd like this." . . .
>
> Then Jesus took the bread and, having given thanks, gave it to those who were seated. He did the same with the fish. All ate as much as they wanted. When the people had eaten their fill, he said to his disciples, "Gather the leftovers so nothing is wasted." They went to work and filled twelve large baskets with leftovers from the five barley loaves.
>
> The people realized that God was at work among them. (John 6:8–14)

The boy surfaces as the hero of the story. All he does is give his lunch to Jesus. He leaves the problem in the hands of the one with the oversight to do something about it.

It might surprise you to know that this boy, though silent in Scripture, was very verbal in life. Indeed, he was the first-century version of a rapper. In my extensive archaeological research, I uncovered this rap song written by the boy with the loaves and fishes. To feel its full impact, don some baggy jeans, turn your baseball cap sideways, and do your best gangsta sway.

Give It Up
by 5 Loaves

I had my loaves and had my fishes
Ready to eat, would be delicious,
But then the master took a look my way
And I knew why I was there that day, to
Give it up . . .
Give it up . . .

You got some struggles, got some fears?
Then listen to me, give me your ears.
Got a question, don't know where to ask it?
Do with it what I did with my basket—
Give it up . . .
Give it up . . .

Jesus got strength you know nothin' of.
His heart for you overflowin' with love.
He fed five thousand with scraps to spare.
He can meet your needs, take away your cares.
Give it up . . .
Give it up . . .

Whether you've got rhythm or not, the point is the same: God is able to do what you can't. So give your problem to Jesus. Don't make the mistake of the disciples. They analyzed, organized, evaluated, and calculated—all without Jesus. The result? They became anxious and bossy.

Go first to Christ. Take your problem and give it up.

FUEL FOR DRAINED DAYS

You're going to run out of gas. We all do. Next time the needle sits on the wrong side of empty, remember: the one who fed the crowds is a prayer away.

God's solution is only a prayer away!

Daylifter

D o you have problems that need to be given to God? If so, take some time to do that now.

When life's problems seem about to overwhelm you, remember this advice from Peter: "Throw the whole weight of your anxieties upon him, for you are his personal concern" (1 Peter 5:7 PHILLIPS).

"Unload all your worries on to him, since he is looking after you" (JB).

"Cast all your anxieties on him, for he cares about you" (RSV).

Translate the message however you want; the point is the same: God's solution is only a prayer away.

CHAPTER 7

Faith for Fear-Filled Days

"Do you think he can?"

"Do you think he cares?"

"Do you think he'll come?"

The questions emerge from the mother's heart. Fear drapes her words and shadows her face.

Her husband stops at the door of their house and looks back into her tired, frightened eyes, then over her shoulder at the figure of his sick daughter lying on the pallet. The girl shivers from fever. The mother shakes from fear. The father shrugs in desperation and answers, "I don't know what he'll do, but I don't know what else to do."

The crowd outside the house parts to let the father

pass. They would on any day. He is the city leader. But they do this day because his daughter is dying.

"Bless you, Jairus," one offers. But Jairus doesn't stop. He hears only the questions of his wife.

"Do you think he can?"

"Do you think he cares?"

"Do you think he'll come?"

Jairus steps quickly down the path through the fishing village of Capernaum. The size of the following crowd increases with every person he passes. They know where Jairus is going. They know whom he seeks. Jairus and the crowd head toward the shore. As they near the water's edge, they spot the teacher, encircled by a multitude. A citizen steps ahead to clear a trail, announcing the presence of the synagogue ruler. Villagers comply. The Red Sea of humanity parts, leaving a people-walled path. Jairus wastes no seconds. "When he saw Jesus, he fell to his knees, beside himself as he begged, 'My dear daughter is at death's door. Come and lay hands on her so she will get well and live.' Jesus went with him, the whole crowd tagging along, pushing and jostling him" (Mark 5:22–24).

Jesus' instant willingness moistens the eyes of Jairus. For the first time in a long time, a sun ray lands on the father's soul. He all but runs as he leads Jesus back to the path toward home. Jairus dares to believe he is moments from a miracle.

Jesus *can* help.

Jesus *does* care.

Jesus is coming.

{ Jesus can help. Jesus does care. Jesus is coming. }

People scatter out of the way and step in behind. Servants rush ahead to inform Jairus's wife. But then, just as suddenly as Jesus started, Jesus stops. Jairus, unaware, takes a dozen more steps before he realizes he's walking alone. The people had stopped when Jesus did. And everyone is trying to make sense of Jesus' question: "Who touched my clothes?" (Mark 5:30 NIV). The sentence triggers a rush of activity. Heads turn toward each other; disciples respond to Christ. Someone moves back so someone else can come forward.

Jairus can't see who. And quite frankly, he doesn't care who. Precious seconds are passing. His precious daughter is passing. Moments ago, he grand-marshaled the Hope Parade. Now he stands on the outside looking in and feels his fragile faith unravel. He looks toward his house and back at Christ and wonders afresh:

I wonder if he can.

I wonder if he cares.

I wonder if he'll come.

We know the questions of Jairus because we've faced the fear of Jairus. His Capernaum is our hospital, principal's office, or lonely room. His dying daughter is our dying academic career, future, or friendship. Jairus is not the last to ask Jesus for a miracle.

We've done the same. With belief weighing barely a feather more than unbelief, we've fallen at Jesus' feet and begged. He replies with hope. His answer delivers fresh light. The cloud parts. The sun shines . . . for a time.

But halfway to the miracle, Jesus stops. The illness returns, the principal frowns, the girl breaks up, the friend stomps away, the parents separate, and we find ourselves with Jairus, on the outside looking in, feeling like a low item on God's to-do list, wondering if Jesus remembers. Wondering if he can, cares, or will come.

Jairus feels a touch on his shoulder. He turns to look into the pale face of a sad servant, who tells him, "Your daughter is dead. Do not trouble the Teacher" (Luke 8:49 NKJV). It's fallen to me on a few occasions to fulfill the task of this servant. To bear death tidings. I've informed a father of the death of his teenage son, my siblings of the death of our dad, more than one child of the death of a parent.

Each announcement is met with silence. Wailing or fainting may soon follow, but the first response is a shock-soaked silence. As if no heart can receive the words and no words can express the heart. No one knows what to say to death.

Was it into such a silence that Jesus urged, "Don't be afraid; just believe" (Mark 5:36 NIV)?

Believe? Jairus might have thought. *Believe what? Believe how? Believe who? My daughter is dead. My wife is distraught. And you, Jesus, well, Jesus, you are late. Had you come when I asked, followed when I led . . . Why did you let my little girl die?*

Jairus had no way of knowing the answer. But we do. Why did Jesus let the girl die? So that two thousand years' worth of strugglers would hear Jesus' response to human tragedy. To all who have stood where Jairus stood and asked what Jairus asked, Jesus says, "Don't be afraid; just believe."

Believe that he can. Believe that he is able to help.

{ *Believe that he can.* }

Note how the story takes a sudden turn. Until this point Jesus has followed the lead of Jairus; now he takes control. He commandeers the scene. He trims his team down to fighting size: "And He permitted no one to follow Him except Peter, James, and John the brother of James" (v. 37 NKJV).

Jesus tells the mourners to simmer down. "When He came in, He said to them, 'Why make this commotion and weep? The child is not dead, but sleeping'" (v. 39 NKJV).

When they mocked him, "He . . . put them all outside" (v. 40 NKJV). The English translation softens the action. The Greek uses a bare-knuckled verb; *ekballo* means to cast out or throw out. Jesus, the temple cleanser and demon caster, rolls up his sleeves. He's the sheriff in the rowdy saloon, placing one hand on a shirt collar and the other on a trouser belt and tossing the troublemaking doubt-stirrers into the street.

He then turns his attention to the body of the girl. He bears the confidence of Einstein adding two plus two, Beethoven playing "Chopsticks," or LeBron James moving in for a three-pointer. Can Jesus call the dead to life? Of course he can.

But does he care? Might he be mighty *and* tender? Have muscle *and* mercy? Does the plight of a twelve-year-old girl in Podunkville appear on the radar screen of heaven?

An earlier moment in the story reveals the answer. It's subtle. You might have missed it. "As soon as Jesus heard the word that was spoken, He said to the ruler of the synagogue, 'Do not be afraid; only believe'" (v. 36 NKJV).

{ *"Do not be afraid; only believe."* }

Jesus heard the servant's words. No one had to tell him about the girl's death. Though separated from Jairus, occupied with the case of the woman who had touched his clothes, encircled by pressing villagers, Jesus never took his ear off the girl's father. Jesus was listening the entire time. He heard. He cared. He cared enough to speak to Jairus's fear, to come to Jairus's home.

> He took the father and the mother of the child, and those who were with Him, and entered where the child was lying. Then He took the child by the hand, and said to her, "Talitha, cumi," which is translated, "Little girl, I say to you, arise." Immediately the girl arose and walked. (5:40–42 NKJV)

A pronouncement from the path would have worked. A declaration from afar would have awakened the girl's heart. But Jesus wanted to do more than raise the dead.

He wanted to show that he not only can and cares, but that he comes.

And sometimes he comes using the hands and heart of a nineteen-year-old girl.

YOUTH WITH A MISSION

Mom for a Day in Mozambique

Veronica Morris, 19, didn't get enough of Africa the first time. After three weeks working with kids in Mozambique, she returned a year later to spend another six months loving, serving, and laughing with the children.

In one of her many experiences, Veronica and the women from the team wrapped the orphanage babies in traditional capalanas, yards of fabric used to carry babies on their mother's backs, and they went to the zoo as "moms" for the day. "It was rather comical to watch," Veronica said. "The first time we tried it the local women sat back, watched us, laughed, and then helped us."

The girl Veronica carried was also named Veronica. She had been sent to the orphanage by her father when she was about a year old so he could care for seven other children after her mother died.

Life in Mozambique is hard. The UN estimates one of every four children dies before he or she reaches five years old, largely due to unsanitary water and malnutrition. Veronica said the orphanage serves as an oasis for children. "The kids long for the Lord," she explained. "Many of them desire to go to Bible school and become teachers, missionaries, or pastors.

"God did so much that made me never want to leave,"

she said. "It broke my heart because the first thing the kids would ask us was, 'What is your name?' and, 'How long are you here for?' I hated having to say, 'Only three weeks.'" But two weeks into the trip, she knew she would be back. "When we were saying goodbye, some of the younger children cried and begged us not to go," she said, "which really made me excited to be able to say, 'I'm coming back.'"

Veronica hopes to pursue a nursing degree after her time in Africa and possibly return to the field.[1]

Jesus may reach the world in the form of a young stranger or speak to us through an old friend. However Jesus comes, he comes to all. He speaks to all. He came to Sean Patrick Jackson.

When Sean volunteered to help with VBS at his church, he was given the assignment of "storyteller." He was terrified of speaking in public and would have to tell the story three times, to three different groups! *What happens if I mess up or forget a line?* he worried. He spent the day of his assignment praying, mostly that he wouldn't mess up, but also that God would be with him. The first group was a little rough. "I forgot some lines, some kids interrupted, and worst of all, it was the biggest group, and the pastor was there," he remembers. "But during one of the breaks, I noticed a young boy smiling at me, and it carried me through." Again, in the second and third groups, there was someone smiling, encouraging Sean, helping his confidence to grow. "It made me think of what I had prayed earlier in the day: 'Jesus, please be with me.' And Jesus, being Jesus, didn't disappoint. He was with me every step of the way."[2]

Sometimes we just need a smile or a word, don't we? And God still gives it. To the terrified. To the overwhelmed. To the downcast. To Jairus the father. To us. He still urges: "Don't be afraid; just believe."

Believe that he can; believe that he cares; believe that he comes. Oh, how we need to believe. Fear steals so much peace from our days.

When ancient sailors sketched maps of the oceans, they disclosed their fears. On the vast unexplored waters, cartographers wrote words such as these:

"Here be dragons."

"Here be demons."

"Here be sirens."

If a map of your world were drawn, would we read such phrases? Over the unknown waters of childhood: "Here be dragons"? Near the sea of your teens: "Here be demons"? Next to the farthermost latitudes of adulthood, will you read: "Here be sirens"?

If so, take heart from the example of Sir John Franklin. He was a master mariner in the days of King Henry V. Distant waters were a mystery to him, just as they were to other navigators. Unlike his colleagues, however, Sir John Franklin was a man of faith. The maps that passed through his possession bore the imprimatur of trust. On them he had crossed out the phrases "Here be dragons," "Here be demons," and "Here be sirens." In their place he wrote the phrase "Here is God."[3]

Mark it down. You will never go where God is not. You may be moving, hiding, waiting in foster care, or lying in a hospital, but—brand this truth on your heart—you can never go where God is not. "I am with you always," Jesus promised (Matthew 28:20 NKJV).

{ *Don't be afraid; just believe.* }

The presence of fear does not mean you have no faith. Fear visits everyone. But make your fear a visitor, not a resident. Hasn't fear taken enough? Enough smiles? Chuckles? Restful nights? Exuberant days? Meet your fears with faith.

Do what my father urged my brother and me to do. Summertime for the Lucado family always involved a trip from West Texas to the Rocky Mountains. (Think Purgatory to Paradise.) My dad loved to fish for trout on the edge of the whitewater rivers. Yet he knew that the currents were dangerous and his sons could be careless. Upon arrival we'd scout out the safe places to cross the river. He'd walk us down the bank until we found a line of stable rocks. He was even known to add one or two to compensate for our short strides.

As we watched, he'd test the stones, knowing that if they held him, they'd hold us. Once on the other side, he'd signal for us to follow.

Does a river of fear run between you and Jesus? Cross over to him. Had Jairus waved Jesus away, death would have taken his hope. If you wave Jesus away, joy will die, laughter will perish, and tomorrow will be buried in today's grave of dread.

Don't make that mistake. Make this day count. Believe he can. Believe he cares. Believe he comes. Don't be afraid. Just believe.

You turn toward God, and he runs toward you.

Daylifter

righten your day by picturing God running toward you. When his people trusted, God blessed. When Peter preached or Paul wrote or Thomas believed, God smiled. But he never *ran*.

That verb was reserved for the story of the prodigal son. "But when he was still a great way off, his father saw him and had compassion, and ran and fell on his neck and kissed him" (Luke 15:20 NKJV).

God runs when he sees the son coming home from the pig trough. When the addict steps out of the alley. When the teen walks away from the party. When the ladder-climbing executive pushes back from the desk, the spiritist turns from idols, the materialist from stuff, the atheist from disbelief, and the elitist from self-promotion . . .

When prodigals trudge up the path, God can't sit still. Heaven's throne room echoes with the sound of slapping sandals and pounding feet, and angels watch in silence as God embraces his child.

Can you imagine the warmth of God's arms around you? Turn to him; you will feel it.

CHAPTER 8

Passion for Purposeless Days

Posted outside the choir rehearsal room was this flyer:

High School Musical:
Oklahoma!
Tryouts next Thursday and Friday

My opportunity at last! If Buddy Holly and Roy Orbison could make the leap from West Texas to the big stage, why couldn't I? I was a high school sophomore brimming with untapped and undiscovered talent. Besides, I already had the boots, hat, and accent. Why not give it a go?

My audition was stellar, until I opened my mouth to sing. The music director covered his ears and placed his head between his knees. Outside the window, a dog began to howl. On the wall, paint began to curl. Still, the director said he might have a spot for me. He asked if I had theater experience. I told him I went to the movies about once a month. That was enough for him. He gave me a script and the page number on which I would find my part. That's right, page number. Not page *numbers*. Page *number*. My part fit on one page. Check that. One paragraph on one page. More accurately, one line in one paragraph on one page.

Decades later, I still remember both words. Having knelt over the body of a just-shot cowboy, I was to lift my head and cry in desperation, "He's daid!" Not, "He's dead," but, "He's d-a-i-d, daid!"

Others might resent such a diminutive role. Not me. Did my words not have purpose? Someone has to announce a stage death. I poured my soul into that line. Why, had you looked closely enough, you might have spotted the tiny tear forming in the corner of my eye.

Rodgers and Hammerstein would have been proud. But, of course, they never knew. When they wrote their story, they weren't thinking of me. But when God wrote his, he was thinking of us all.

What's your part? Don't think for a moment that you don't have one. God "shaped each person in turn" (Psalm 33:15). "Each of us is an original" (Galatians 5:26). He cast you in his play, wrote you into his story. No assignment too small. No lines too brief. He has a definite purpose for your life. Fulfill it and enjoy fulfillment. Play the part God prepared for you, and get ready for some great days.

What's your part?

What about Simon from Cyrene? He played a supporting role in the journey to Jesus' crucifixion. As Jesus struggled toward that infamous hill of Golgotha, a Roman guard appointed Simon to help Jesus carry the cross. In playing his part, Simon did literally what God calls us to do figuratively—take up the cross and follow Jesus. "If any of you want to be my followers, you must forget about yourself. You must take up your cross and follow me" (Mark 8:34 CEV).

The phrase "take up your cross" has not fared well through the generations. Ask for an example, and you'll hear answers like, "My cross is my stepmother," "my chores," "my cranky teacher," or the "boring preacher." The cross, we assume, is any troubling affliction or personal hassle. My thesaurus agrees. It lists the following synonyms for cross: *frustration, trying situation, snag, hitch,* and *drawback.* To take up the cross is to put up with a personal challenge. God, we think, passes out crosses the way a warden hands out shovels to the chain gang. No one wants one. Each one gets one. Everybody has a cross to bear, and we might as well get used to it.

But, come on. Is Jesus reducing the cross to hassles and headaches? Calling us to quit complaining about the fly in the soup or the pain in the neck? The cross means so much more. It is God's tool of redemption, instrument of salvation—proof of his love for people. To take up the cross, then, is to take up Christ's burden for the people of the world.

Though our crosses are similar, none are identical. "If any of you want to be my followers, you must forget about yourself. You must take up *your cross* each day and follow me" (Luke 9:23 CEV).

We each have our own cross to carry—our individual callings. Yours awaits you like a snug-fitting shirt. We all know the discomfort of poorly fitted clothes. Being the baby in my family, I inherited my share of hand-me-downs from my brother. They covered my flesh but failed to fit my body. Tight cloth pinched my shoulders, and the collar draped on my neck. It was a fine day when Mom decided to buy me shirts that fit.

It's an even sweeter day when you discover your God-designed task. It fits. It matches your passions and enlists your gifts and talents. Want to blow the cloud cover off your gray day? Accept God's direction.

{ Accept God's direction. }

John Bentley did. He carries a cross for Chinese orphans. This Christian lawyer lives in Beijing, where he and his wife oversee an orphanage for abandoned babies. Some years ago, a mother deposited a newborn, dressed in burial clothes, in a nearby field. No note, no explanation, just the Chinese equivalent of $1.25: the price of a burial. The mother had abandoned her child. One examination revealed why. The child was severely burned from head to toe.

The Bentleys could not let the child die. They not only nursed the boy back to health, but they adopted him as their son. They carry the cross of Christ for the children of China.

Michael Landon Jr. carries one for the film industry. He's uniquely qualified to do so. His dad, Michael Landon, was famous for his roles on popular TV shows such as *Bonanza* and *Little House on the Prairie*. Michael Landon Jr. grew up around the entertainment business. When Christ claimed his nineteen-year-old heart, he set out to influence the world of entertainment. He pours daily energy and credibility into one task: creating redemptive films. Few have the training or the experience to do what he does. But since Michael has both, he daily shoulders the cross of Christ for Hollywood.

Joseph Rojas, lead singer of Seventh Day Slumber, bears the heavy cross for curbing addiction. He tells his own story of hitting rock bottom—stealing money from his mom to buy drugs and intentionally ingesting a lethal dose of cocaine. As he lay in the back of an ambulance, his mom screaming for God to save his life, a powerful feeling hit him, and he asked Jesus to save him. Joseph now shares his story at every Seventh Day Slumber show and estimates that over twenty thousand people have responded to altar calls as a result. After the shows, Joseph and his band stay until they have personally spoken with everyone wanting to talk with them. Seventh Day Slumber makes the most of their opportunities to connect with youth and remind them of the one who loves them.[1]

"The Lord has assigned to each his task" (1 Corinthians 3:5 NIV). What is yours? What is your unique call, assignment, mission?

A trio of questions might help.

In what directions has God taken you? Tally up the experiences unique to you. "Don't act thoughtlessly, but try to find out and do whatever the Lord wants you to" (Ephesians 5:17 TLB). In what culture have you been raised? To what lifestyles have you been exposed? Your past is a signpost to your future. Ask Moses. His Egyptian childhood experiences prepared him to stand before Pharaoh. David grew up herding sheep. Not bad training for one called to pastor a nation. Paul's pedigree as a Roman citizen likely extended his life and his ministry. Your past is no accident.

What about your burdens? *What needs has God revealed to you?* What makes your heart race and blood pump? Not everyone weeps when you do. Not everyone hurts like you do. Heed the hurts and passions of your heart. We each "run with patience the particular race that God has set before us" (Hebrews 12:1 TLB). Do you know the race God has set before you?

What abilities has God given to you? "Christ has given each of us special abilities" (Ephesians 4:7 TLB). What comes easy to you? Some of you are good with numbers. Others are good with people. You excel at something and do so with comparatively little effort. Daniel Sharp grew up at the church where I serve. As part of his college education, he moved to Moscow to study calculus, electricity, magnetism, and poetry—in Russian. He found the courses so fun that he e-mailed his parents, "Can't anyone do this?" I don't think so. But the fact that Daniel can says something about his unique call in life.[2]

Something comes easy for you as well. Identify it! "Make a careful exploration of who you are" (Galatians 6:4).

Direction. Need. Ability. Your spiritual DNA. You at your best. You and your cross.

> ## Direction. Need. Ability. Your spiritual DNA.

While none of us is called to carry the sin of the world (Jesus did that), all of us can carry a burden for the world. By the way, this is a wonderful burden. Jesus said, "The load I give you to carry is light" (Matthew 11:30 NCV). The cross is a good weight, a sweet debt. Test this truth. Visit a retirement home with a group of friends. See if you don't leave happier than when you entered. Help teach in a preschool class. See if you don't learn more than they do. Dedicate a Saturday to helping in a homeless shelter. You'll discover another truth: as you help others face their days, you put life into your own. Daniel Kent rediscovers this truth every day.

NOBLESVILLE DAILY TIMES

Student Clicks with Seniors, Creates a Way to Help

by Katie Wampler

He just may be the youngest board member Carmel's PrimeLife Enrichment has ever seen. But according to Executive Director Sandy Stewart, sophomore Daniel Kent displays an uncommon passion for service. "He's an inspiration," she said.

Kent doesn't see himself that way. He simply saw a need and acted to fill it. "When I wake up, I really am looking forward to volunteering," Kent said. "It is absolutely fun."

It all began as Kent prepared for his freshman year. He was volunteering at a public library to teach computer skills to senior citizens. A gentleman Kent had been teaching approached him and said he had a friend in a nursing home who needed to learn to use computers but could not come to the library for the class.

"I really wanted to help his friend," Kent said. "So I looked around for an organization that could teach Internet skills." But Kent found none.

"After that, Senior Connects began to form, and here we are today."

Before he was even in high school, he formed what is today a 250-member not-for-profit business serving seniors in nursing homes and assisted living centers across central Indiana, from Indianapolis to Carmel and Westfield. The Senior Connects staff usually spends Saturdays and holidays off school at facilities across central Indiana, Kent said.

And the business continues to grow.

Kent's achievement has caught national attention. This year CNN named Kent one of nine Do Something BRICK

Award winners nationwide, an honor the broadcasting network likens to the "Oscars of youth service awards." Along with the recognition, Kent received a $10,000 scholarship for providing computer access to 61 assisted living facilities and nursing homes, serving more than 10,000 residents statewide.

Sandy Stewart adds, "(Kent) is just a remarkable young man who identified a need in the community and did something about it."

Kent said he hopes to turn the company into a not-for-profit franchise and establish multiple locations statewide that employ his Senior Connects philosophy.

In the end, Kent feels collaboration is key.

"It's true that one person can make a difference. But through teamwork, we can change the world."[3]

Daniel Kent has done enough in his eighteen years to make many accomplished adults feel like selfish slugs. So get going now. Use your spiritual DNA to tune in to your calling and, regardless of your age or resources, find a way to pursue it.

Check your vital signs. Something stirs you. Some purpose brings passion to your voice, conviction to your face, and direction to your step. Isolate and embrace it. Nothing gives a day a greater chance than a good wallop of passion.

Inject passion into purposeless days by doing something for someone else!

Daylifter

sk God to inject his passion in your day.

Pray for every person you pass. Don't grumble on the long bus ride or complain in crowded hallways. These are prayer moments. Intercede for each person you see, "praying always with all prayer" (Ephesians 6:18 NKJV). Imitate Epaphras, whom Paul said was "always laboring fervently for you in prayers" (Colossians 4:12 NKJV). He labored, strove, worked in prayers. I'm seeing a strained face, tearful cheeks, clenched hands.

Stir spiritual dialogue. At the right time, with the right heart, ask your friends and family, "What do you think happens after we die?" "What is your view of God?" Jesus asked such questions: "Who do you say I am?" (Mark 8:29 NIV). Let's ask them too.

Love because God loves. People can be tough to love. Love them anyway. "He who loves God must love his brother also" (1 John 4:21 NKJV).

Who can you pray for, talk to, love . . . today?

CHAPTER 9

Service for Fork-in-the-Road Days

Dan Mazur considered himself lucky. Most other people would have considered him crazy. He stood within a two-hour hike of the summit of Mount Everest, just a thousand feet from realizing a lifelong dream.

Every year, the fittest adventurers on earth set their sights on the twenty-nine-thousand-foot peak. Every year, some die in the effort. The top of Everest isn't known for its hospitality. Climbers call the realm above twenty-six thousand feet "the death zone."

Temperatures hover below zero. Sudden blizzards stir blinding snow. The atmosphere is oxygen starved. Corpses dot the mountaintop. A British climber had died ten days prior to Mazur's attempt. Forty climbers who could have helped chose not to do so. They passed him on the way to the summit.

Everest can be cruel.

Still, Mazur felt lucky. He and two colleagues were within eyesight of the top. Years of planning. Six weeks of climbing, and now at 7:30 a.m., May 25, 2006, the air was still, morning sun brilliant, energy and hopes high. That's when a flash of color caught Mazur's eye: a bit of yellow fabric on the ridgetop. He first thought it was a tent. He soon saw it was a person, a man precariously perched on an eight-thousand-foot razor-edge rock. His gloves were off, jacket unzipped, hands exposed, chest bare. Oxygen deprivation can swell the brain and stir hallucinations. Mazur knew this man had no idea where he was, so he walked toward him and called out.

"Can you tell me your name?"

"Yes," the man answered, sounding pleased. "I can. My name is Lincoln Hall."

Mazur was shocked. He recognized this name. Twelve hours earlier he'd heard the news on the radio: "Lincoln Hall is dead on the mountain. His team has left his body on the slope."

And yet, after spending the night in twenty-below chill and oxygen-stingy air, Lincoln Hall was still alive. Mazur was face-to-face with a miracle.

He was also face-to-face with a choice. A rescue attempt had profound risks. The descent was already treacherous, even more so with the dead weight of a dying man. Besides, how long would Hall survive? No one knew. The three climbers might sacrifice their Everest summit for naught. They had to choose: abandon their dream or abandon Lincoln Hall.

They chose to abandon their dream. The three turned their backs on the peak and inched their way down the mountain.[1]

Their decision to save Hall's life stirs a great question: Would we do the same? Surrender ambition to save someone else? Set aside our dreams to rescue another climber? Turn our backs on our personal mountaintops so someone else might live?

We make such fork-in-the-road decisions daily. Not on Everest with adventurers, but in homes with parents and siblings, in schools with friends, in churches with fellow believers. We regularly face subtle yet significant decisions, all of which fall under the category of who comes first: Do they or do I?

{ Who comes first: Do they or do I? }

When the parent chooses the best school for the children over a career-advancing transfer.

When the student eats lunch with the neglected kids rather than the cool ones.

When the granddaughter spends her Saturdays playing checkers with her aging grandfather.

When a girl forfeits a trip to the Olympics for her best friend . . .

No, really. It happened when Kay Poe and Esther Kim, best friends, made it to the finals for tae kwon do at the U.S. Olympic Team Trials. But in her semifinal match, Kay dislocated her kneecap. It was generally assumed that Esther would easily defeat Kay and gain the ultimate privilege of competing in the Olympics. Esther Kim, however, knew there was no way that would happen. Instead of defeating her friend in an unfair match, Esther forfeited, sending Kay to the Olympic games.[2]

When you turn away from personal dreams for the sake of others—as Esther Kim selflessly did—you are, in Christ's words, denying yourself. "If any of you wants to be my follower, you must turn from your selfish ways, take up your cross, and follow me" (Matthew 16:24 NLT).

Erica Reese was anything but selfish. She took up a cross and followed a calling for the sake of others. Along with her family and friends, Erica dedicated a tremendous effort to making an incalculable difference in the lives of children half a world away—children who may have viewed those in the United States as less than friendly and who probably had never heard of Christ and his cross.

ELGIN EAGLE

Niceville Kids Collect Gifts for Iraqi Kids

by Sheila Vaughen

Erica and her mother Diana Reese generated approximately $10,000 worth of donations for children of an Iraqi schoolhouse near Balad Air Base in Iraq. The donations of school supplies and money went to assembling, filling, packaging, and mailing 200 handcrafted bags containing crayons, markers, drawing tablets, and toys.

Named Operation Iraqi Friendship, the project was spearheaded by Ms. Reese, Erica, her 12-year-old brother Tim, sister Bailey, 7, and family friend Brad Steinke, 15. Numerous other Niceville kids put in countless hours for the operation, which got off the ground largely because of Maj. Keith Peloquin during his Iraq deployment.

A friend of Ms. Reese, Major Peloquin was instrumental in establishing a contact with the Iraqi school. Just before his deployment to Iraq was ending, Major Peloquin passed the project over to Lt. Col. Craig King. Colonel King, who has a daughter at Niceville High School, is still involved in distributing the goods to the children. He is convinced the project has filled an important purpose.

"This is clearly the right thing to do . . . these children live in an environment where they have to make some adult-sized decisions at an early age. They'll never forget that American kids and troops went out of their way to help them out," Colonel King said.

Ms. Reese said that according to Major Peloquin, when the Iraqi kids first held the supplies, their first instinct was to share.

"The kids were each given a box of crayons, but the Iraqi kids would only take one crayon because that's all they were used to," she said. "We were told about kids who would take just one crayon and break it in two, giving the other half to a child next to them."

Ms. Reese said the Airmen in Iraq reported that when the Iraqi kids colored pictures with their new crayons, they would use just one color because they had never before had a whole box of crayons to use as they pleased.

Operation Iraqi Friendship was born out of the enjoyment experienced by Erica, Tim, Bailey, and Brad when they sent care packages to soldiers and Airmen deployed to support Operation Iraqi Freedom.

Just after Christmas, the care packages for American troops transformed into friendship-building donations for Iraqi school children.

While the project has already impacted the Iraqi students, it's not over yet. Now Ms. Reese and the kids are gathering shoes because they learned that 80 percent of the Iraqi kids were without. They are also collecting baby clothes and other personal goods.

The kids who spearheaded the operation seem to have learned some valuable lessons from their philanthropy.

"We really learned how much we take for granted here," Tim said.

"It was a fun thing to do, just knowing how much we helped some little kids," Brad added.[3]

I'm sure we'll never know the full impact Operation Iraqi Friendship had on those children. An act of such incomprehensible generosity—*more than one crayon?*—at such a young age no doubt had an immeasurable effect on the children of the Iraqi schoolhouse, their families, and their society as a whole . . . all because one group took up a cross for them.

This brings us to the most surprising ingredient of a great day: self-denial.

Don't we assume just the opposite? Great days emerge from the soil of self-indulgence, self-expression, and self-celebration. So pamper yourself; indulge yourself; promote yourself. But deny yourself? When was the last time you read this ad copy: "Go ahead. Deny yourself and have the time of your life!"?

Jesus could have written the words. He often goes countercultural, calling us down rather than up, telling us to zig when society says to zag.

In his economy,

- the least are the greatest (Luke 9:48);
- the last will be first (Mark 9:35);
- the chosen seats are the forgotten seats (Luke 14:8–9).

He tells us to honor others above ourselves (Romans 12:10), consider others better than ourselves (Philippians 2:3), turn the other cheek, give away our coats, and walk the second mile (Matthew 5:39–41).

That last instruction surely struck a raw nerve in the Jewish psyche. "Whoever compels you to go one mile, go with him two" (Matthew 5:41 NKJV). Jesus' fellow citizens lived under foreign rule. They were sloshing through centuries-old swamp: oppressed by pagans, looking for the Messiah to deliver them.

Some responded by selling out, working the system to their own advantage. Others got out. Still others decided to fight back.

Three options: sell out, get out, or fight back.

Jesus introduced a fourth. Serve. Serve the ones who hate you; forgive the ones who hurt you. Take the lowest place, not the highest; seek to serve, not to be served. Retaliate, not in kind but in kindness. He created what we might deem the Society of the Second Mile.

Roman soldiers could legally require Jewish citizens to carry their load for one mile.[4] With nothing more than a command, they could order a farmer out of his field or a merchant out of his shop.

In such a case, Jesus said, "Give more than requested." Go two. At the end of one mile, keep going. Surprise the sandals off the soldier by saying, "I haven't done enough for you. I'm going a second mile." Do more than demanded. And do so with joy and grace!

{ *Give more than requested.* }

The Society of the Second Mile still exists. Its members surrender Everest-level ambitions so they can help weary climbers find safety.

We have a second-mile servant in our church. By profession he is an architect. By passion, a servant. He arrives an hour or so prior to each worship service and makes his rounds through the men's restrooms. He wipes the sinks, cleans the mirrors, checks the toilets, and picks up paper off the floor. No one asked him to do the work; very few people are aware he does it. He tells no one and requests nothing in return. He belongs to the Society of the Second Mile.

Or consider seventeen-year-old Rashaeda Nykwae Bryant, a third-generation second-miler. Inspired by her grandmother, she founded a nonprofit organization called

PEACE: Pupils Engaging and Achieving in Community Excellence. Rashaeda credits her grandmother for molding her into the person she is today, saying, "She always encouraged me to continue on and do what no other has done." To go that second mile.[5]

Another second-miler serves in our children's ministry. She creates crafts and take-home gifts for four-year-olds. Completing the craft is not enough, however. She has to give it a second-mile touch. When a class followed the theme "Walking in the Steps of Jesus," she made cookies in the shape of a foot and, in second-mile fashion, painted toenails on each cookie. Who does that?

Second-milers do. They clean bathrooms, encourage community excellence, decorate cookies, and build playrooms in their houses. At least Bob and Elsie did. They built an indoor pool, bought a Ping-Pong table and a foosball game. They created a playroom paradise.

Not unusual, you say? Oh, I forgot to mention their ages. They did this in their seventies. They did this because they loved the lonely youth of downtown Miami. Bob didn't swim. Elsie didn't play Ping-Pong. But the kids of immigrant Cubans did. And Bob could be seen each week driving his Cadillac through Little Havana, picking up the teens other people forgot.

The Society of the Second Mile. Let me tell you how to spot its members. They don't wear badges or uniforms; they wear smiles. They have discovered the secret. The joy is found in the extra effort. The sweetest satisfaction lies not in climbing your own Everest but in helping other climbers.

{ The joy is found in the extra effort. }

Second-milers read Jesus' statement "It is more blessed to give than to receive" (Acts 20:35 NIV) and nod their heads. When they hear the instruction, "If your first concern is to look after yourself, you'll never find yourself" (Matthew 10:39), they understand. They've discovered this truth: "Self-help is no help at all. Self-sacrifice is the way, *my* way, to finding yourself, your true self" (Luke 9:24).

The real reward rests at the base of the second-mile post.

Think of it this way. Imagine yourself facing a sink of dirty dishes. You don't want to wash them. You'd rather play with your friends or watch television. But your mom has made it clear: clean the dishes.

You groan, moan, and wonder how you might go about placing yourself up for adoption. Then, from who knows where, a wacky idea strikes you. What if you surprise your mom by cleaning not just the dishes but the entire kitchen? You begin to smile. *I'll sweep the floor and wipe down the cabinets. Maybe reorganize the refrigerator!* And from some unknown source comes a shot of energy, a surge of productivity. A dull task becomes an adventure. Why? Liberation! You've passed from slave to volunteer.

This is the joy of the second mile.

Have you found it? Your day moves with the speed of an iceberg and the excitement of a quilting tournament. You do what is required—math problems and one chapter in literature—but no more. You are reliable, dependable, and quite likely bored. You dream of Fridays, snow days, a different family, or a different school—when maybe all you need is a different attitude. Make this day count.

Daily do a deed for which you cannot be repaid.

In the final days of Jesus' life, he shared a meal with his friends Lazarus, Martha, and Mary. Within the week he would feel the sting of the Roman whip, the point of the thorny crown, and the iron of the executioner's nail. But on this evening, he felt the love of three friends.

For Mary, however, giving the dinner was not enough. "Mary came in with a jar of very expensive aromatic oils, anointed and massaged Jesus' feet, and then wiped them with her hair. The fragrance of the oils filled the house" (John 12:3).

One-milers among the group, like Judas, criticized the deed as wasteful. Not Jesus. He received the gesture as an extravagant demonstration of love, a friend surrendering her most treasured gift. As Jesus hung on the cross, we wonder, did he detect the fragrance on his skin?

Follow Mary's example.

There is an elderly man in your community who just lost his wife. An hour of your time would mean the world to him.

Some kids in your city have no dad. No father takes them to movies or baseball games. Maybe you can. They can't pay you back. They can't even afford the popcorn or sodas. But they'll smile like a cantaloupe slice at your kindness.

Or how about this one? Down the hall from your

bedroom is a person who shares your last name. Shock that person with kindness. Something outlandish. Your homework done with no complaints. A bowl of cereal in bed. A long overdue thank-you letter. A clean room, just because.

Want to snatch a day from the bonds of boredom? Do overgenerous deeds, acts beyond reimbursement. Kindness without compensation. Do a deed for which you cannot be repaid.

Here's another idea. *Get over yourself.*

Moses did. One of history's foremost leaders was "a very humble man, more humble than anyone else on the face of the earth" (Numbers 12:3 NIV).

Mary did. When Jesus made her womb his home, she did not boast; she simply confessed: "I'm the Lord's maid, ready to serve" (Luke 1:38).

John the Baptist did. Though a blood relative of God on earth, he made this choice: "This is the assigned moment for him to move into the center, while I slip off to the sidelines" (John 3:30).

Most of all, Jesus did. He "was given a position 'a little lower than the angels'" (Hebrews 2:9 NLT).

If Jesus chose the servants' quarters, can't we?

We're important, but not essential; valuable, but not indispensable. We have a part in the play, but we are not the leading role. A song to sing, but we are not the featured voice.

God is.

He did well before our births; he'll do fine after our deaths. He started it all, sustains it all, and will bring it all to a glorious climax. In the meantime, we have this high privilege: to surrender personal Everests, discover the thrill of the doubled distance, do deeds for which we cannot be paid, seek problems that others avoid, deny ourselves, take up our crosses, and follow Christ.

Lincoln Hall survived the trip down Mount Everest. Thanks to Dan Mazur, he lived to be reunited with his wife and sons in New Zealand. A television reporter asked Lincoln's wife what she thought of the rescuers, the men who surrendered their summit to save her husband's life. She tried to answer, but the words stuck in her throat. After several moments and with tear-filled eyes, she offered, "Well, there's one amazing human being. And the other men with him. The world needs more people like that."[6]

May we be numbered among them.

Daily do a deed for which you cannot be repaid.

Daylifter

*Teach us how short our lives really
are so that we may be wise.*
Psalm 90:12 NCV

If today were your last day of life, how would you spend it? Facing death is bitter medicine, but most of us could use a spoonful. Most of us could benefit from a reminder. You don't want one, and I can't say I enjoy giving one, but we need to know: we have one less day to live than yesterday.

If today were your last, would you do what you're doing? Or would you love more, give more, forgive more? Then do it! Forgive and give as if it were your last opportunity. Love like there's no tomorrow, and if tomorrow comes, love again.

CHAPTER 10

Grace for Guilty Days

What the thief sees. Defiant faces lining a cobbled path. Men spitting in disgust, women turning in contempt.

What the thief hears. Pounding. Soldiers grunt as they lift the cross. The base thuds as it falls into the hole.

What the thief feels. Pain. Breathtaking, pulse-stopping pain. Every fiber on fire.

What the thief hears. Groans. Death. Just the harsh chords of death.

Pain. Death. He sees them; he hears them. But then the thief sees and hears something else: "Father, forgive them, for they do not know what they do" (Luke 23:34 NKJV).

A flute sings on a battlefield. A rain cloud blocks a desert sun. A rose blossoms on death ridge.

Jesus prays on a Roman cross.

Here is how the thief reacts: mockery. "He saved

others—he can't save himself! King of Israel, is he? Then let him get down from that cross. . . . He did claim to be God's Son, didn't he?" (Matthew 27:42–43).

But Jesus refuses to retaliate. And the thief sees, for the first time that day (for the first time in how many days?), kindness. Not darting glances or snarling lips but patient tolerance.

The thief softens. He stops mocking Christ and then attempts to stop the mocking of Christ. "We deserve this, but not him," he confesses to the crook on the other cross. "He did nothing to deserve this" (Luke 23:41). The thief senses he's close to a man heaven-bound and requests a recommendation: "Jesus, remember me when you enter your kingdom" (v. 42).

> { "We deserve this, but not him." }

And Jesus, who made and makes an eternal life out of inviting outcasts into his kingdom, issues this grace-drenched reply: "Don't worry, I will. Today you will join me in paradise" (v. 43).

And the bad day of the bad man is met with the gracious gift of a mercy-giving God.

What does the thief see now? He sees the God who wrote the book on grace. The God who coaxed Adam and Eve out of the bushes, murderous Moses out of the desert. The God who didn't give up on Elijah, though Elijah gave up on God. This is what the thief sees.

What does he hear? He hears what fugitive Moses heard in the desert, depressed Elijah heard in the desert, the storm-tossed disciples heard after the wind stopped, the blind man heard when Jesus found him on the street. He hears the official language of Christ: grace. Undeserved. Unexpected. Grace. "Today you will join me in paradise" (v. 43).

Paradise. The intermediate heaven. The home of the righteous until the return of Christ. The Tree of Life is there. Saints are there. God is there. And now the thief, who began the day in a Roman jail, will be there.

With Jesus. "Today you will join me." No back-door entrance. No late-night arrival. Paradise knows neither night nor second-class citizens. The thief enters the gate on Jesus' red carpet.

Today. Immediately. No Purgatory purging. No Hades rehab. Grace comes like a golden sunrise, illuminating the thief's dark day. Execution hill becomes a mountain of change.

Perhaps you could use some of the same. Yesterday's mistakes play the role of the Roman death squad: they escort you up the calvary of shame. Faces of the past line the trail. Voices declare your crimes as you pass:

You neglected your education!

You lied to your father and me!

You promised you'd do better!

You're soon nailed to the cross of your mistakes. Dumb mistakes. What do you see? Death. What do you feel? Guilt. Shame. What do you hear?

Ah, this is the question. What do you hear? Can you

hear Jesus above the accusers? He promises, "Today you will join me in paradise."

Today. This day. In the stink of it, the throes of it, Jesus makes a miracle out of it.

Austin Atkinson became one of those miracles. Like the thief, he faced death, saw it, heard it, smelled it. But also like the thief, he was spared by God's never-ending grace.

CAMPUS LIFE

Why Did I Survive?

by Austin Atkinson, as told to Christy Heitger-Casbon

The night started out innocently enough. A few friends and I were hanging out playing video games. Then my buddy Pete* showed up with some vodka. Within an hour we were all pretty wasted and our small "party" had gotten out of hand.

Josh cranked the music and then grabbed his lighter so we could all try "breathing fire." We took turns spitting vodka and tried lighting it on fire as it left our mouths. But no one could do it.

Then Josh thought it would be cool to get in a circle, pour gasoline in the middle and make a "circle of fire." We watched as he doused the gravel driveway with gasoline.

"You need more over here!" I shouted. I grabbed the container of gas away from Josh, carelessly drenching my shirt and pants.

"Man, you reek!" Pete laughed.

Josh knelt down on the gravel and clicked his lighter several times.

Foop, foop—sssssshhh. Our ring of fire was born. We high-fived one another and celebrated by opening a second bottle of liquor. Feeling pretty wasted, I plopped down on a chair.

"I've got a killer idea," Josh said.

He then poured gasoline all over the plastic chair sitting beside me. A moment later I heard the flick of Josh's lighter, then *swooosh!* The chair was ablaze.

I could feel the heat of the flames. I started to get up so I could move away from the burning chair, but I looked down to see flames ignite my gas-soaked shirt and pants.

Panicked, I jumped up and started screaming and running. No matter which I way I turned, red-hot flames chased me.

"Drop and roll!" Josh yelled.

I rolled for what seemed like an eternity. Then I heard Josh shout, "You're good! It's out, man!"

It didn't feel that way to me. I felt like I'd been swimming in a sea of bubbling lava. That was my last memory until waking up in the hospital.

A nurse told me that I had been rushed to the hospital three weeks earlier with 35 percent of my body covered in third-degree burns. I knew I had messed up big time. It was totally stupid both to drink and to mess around with fire.

Along with regular visits from my parents and friends, my friend Michelle dropped by the hospital several times. We usually talked about movies or music. But one afternoon the conversation turned in a different direction.

"You're gonna be OK," Michelle said softly.

"How do you know?" I asked.

"I've been praying for you," she said.

Awkward silence filled the room.

"Austin, you almost died," Michelle nearly whispered. "But God has given you another shot at life—a chance to make better choices from now on."

Through physical therapy over the next several months, I made great improvements. I learned to walk, write and even drive.

On the one-year anniversary of the accident, I parked my car in front of Josh's house and sat in silence. Horrific images flashed across my mind. My stomach knotted, and my body shuddered as I tried to shake off the memories.

Then I took a deep breath and bowed my head in prayer, thanking God for my second chance at life and for my new life with him. Suddenly my anxiety melted away and I was filled with peace—the kind of peace that only God's love can bring.

*Names changed[1]

When Austin thought his life was over, God showed him a new beginning—ah, the glory of grace. When others nail you to the cross of your past, he swings open the door to your future. Paradise. Jesus treats your guilt-filled days with grace.

He'll take your guilt if you'll ask him. All he awaits is your request. The words of the thief will do. "We deserve this, but not him—he did nothing."

We are wrong. He is right.

We sin. He is the Savior.

We need grace. Jesus can give it.

{ We need grace. Jesus can give it. }

So ask him, "Remember me when you enter your kingdom."

And when you do, the one who spoke then will speak again. "Today you will join me in paradise."[2]

You may have messed up yesterday. Maybe you said the wrong words, went the wrong direction, went out with the wrong person, reacted the wrong way. You spoke when you should have listened, walked when you should have waited, judged when you should have trusted, indulged when you should have resisted.

You messed up yesterday. But you'll mess up more if you let yesterday's mistakes sabotage today's attitude. God's mercies are new every morning. Receive them.

Learn a lesson from the Cascade forests of Washington State. Some of its trees are hundreds of years old, far surpassing the typical life span of fifty to sixty years. One leaf-laden patriarch dates back seven centuries! What makes the difference? Daily drenching rains. Deluges keep the ground moist, the trees wet, and the lightning impotent.[3]

Lightning strikes you as well. Thunderbolts of regret can ignite and consume you if you don't counteract them with downpours of God's grace, daily washings of forgiveness. Once a year won't do. Once a month is insufficient. Weekly showers leave you dry. Sporadic mistings leave you combustible. You need a solid soaking every day. "The Lord's love never ends; his mercies never stop. They are new every morning" (Lamentations 3:22–23 NCV).

> God's mercies are new every morning.
> Receive them. Every morning!

Daylifter

Next time your day goes south, here is what you do. Steep yourself in the grace of God. Saturate your day in his love. Marinate your mind in his mercy. He has settled your accounts, paid your debt. "Christ carried our sins in his body on the cross" (1 Peter 2:24 NCV).

When you lose your temper with a friend, Christ intervenes: "I paid for that." When you tell a lie and all of heaven groans, your Savior speaks up: "My death covered that sin." As you gloat, covet, or judge, Jesus stands before the tribunal of heaven and points to the blood-streaked cross. "I've already made provision. I've taken away the sins of the world."

What a gift he has given you. You've won the greatest lottery in the history of humanity, and you didn't even pay for the ticket! Your soul is secure; your salvation guaranteed. Your name is written in the only book that matters. You're only a few sand grains in the hourglass from a tearless, graveless, painless existence. What more do you need?

Thinking About . . . Making Every Day Count

Student and Group Study Guide

Chapter 1: Make Every Day Count

1. What are some of the things that can really mess up your day?

2. If everyone reacted to bad days the way you do, what would the world be like?

3. God tells us to "rejoice and be glad" (Psalm 118:24 NKJV) in each day he has made. How can you rejoice even on the bad days?

4. In what ways could God use a bad day to strengthen your faith?

5. When you see someone else stuck in a bad day, what can you do or say to help them through?

Chapter 2: Gratitude for Ungrateful Days

1. What are some "favorite things" that you are most grateful for in your life?

2. What are some of the least favorite things in your life? Could focusing on God's grace change the way you think about these things?

3. How do negative thoughts affect your day? Your energy? Your attitude?

4. Are there things about yourself that you don't like? How do you think God sees those things?

5. What does "take every thought captive so that it is obedient to Christ" (2 Corinthians 10:5 God's Word) mean to you?

Chapter 3: Forgiveness for Sour Days

1. If God took a tour of your heart right now, what would he find? Are there things you need to clean out?

2. God's ultimate goal is to make you into the image of Christ. Is something keeping you from looking like Christ?

3. If other people forgave you the same way you forgive, what would that look like?

4. Do you still feel guilty about something you've already been forgiven for? Why do you think that is?

5. How does it feel to know that God sacrificed his own Son in order for you to be forgiven?

Chapter 4: Peace for Stressed-Out Days

1. What are some things that stress you out and make you worry?

2. How do you usually handle worry and stress?

3. What do you think about the phrase "God meets daily needs daily and miraculously"? How could this phrase help you turn your worries over to God?

4. Could "wanting less" take away some of the worry and stress from your life?

5. Do you have some huge task looming over you? How could you break it into manageable parts?

Chapter 5: Hope for Catastrophic Days

1. Does something have you "bumped off track" right now?

2. How can you let God help you get back in the race? How can you allow God to keep you in the race?

3. How can getting "bumped off track" sometimes put you "right on target"?

4. On the Friday of the crucifixion, 80 percent of Jesus' words were to God. When you are having a tough day, what percentage of your words and thoughts are to God?

5. Think about a past catastrophic moment. Can you now see God's presence and plan working through that time?

Chapter 6: Fuel for Drained Days

1. Are there certain situations, relationships, or activities that really drain you?

2. Where do you turn to get refueled? Do you turn to God?

3. To whom do you first take your problems? Is it God? If not, why not?

4. What might happen if you prayed about a problem before you tried to fix it?

5. Do you believe that God has your best interests at heart?

6. Finish this sentence: *In my life, God is able to . . .*

Chapter 7: Faith for Fear-Filled Days

1. Write down your thoughts on each of these phrases:

- Jesus *can* help.
- Jesus *does* care.
- Jesus *is* coming.

2. What does the phrase "Do not be afraid; only believe" mean to you?

3. What are the dragons in your life?

4. How can God chase away those dragons for you?

5. How does it feel to know that God runs to you when you turn to him?

Chapter 8: Passion for Purposeless Days

1. Is there really such a thing as a purposeless day? What are some things you can do to bring God into those days that might seem purposeless?

2. What part in his kingdom do you feel God has given you?

3. Are you playing your part with all your heart?

4. Think about all the experiences of your life so far. Do you see that God has taken you in a certain direction?

5. What are the needs around you that truly touch your heart? Could one of those be your cross to carry for God?

6. How could you use the talents and abilities God has given you to meet those needs?

Chapter 9: Service for Fork-in-the-Road Days

1. What are some fork-in-the-road decisions you face?

2. What helps you choose to put God and others before yourself?

3. How do you feel about giving up your personal dreams for someone else—like Dan Mazur and Esther Kim did? Would it be easier to give up your dreams for a friend or for a stranger?

4. What does the "least are the greatest" mean to you?

5. How can you go the second mile in your life?

6. Are there some ways in which you need to "get over yourself"?

Chapter 10: Grace for Guilty Days

1. In what ways are you like the thief on the cross?

2. What are the times when you most need the grace of Jesus?

3. Are there things you feel guilty about that you need to give to Jesus?

4. Why is it sometimes hard to accept God's mercy and forgiveness?

5. What does the promise "the Lord's love never ends" mean for your life?

Notes

Chapter 1

1. My thanks to Judith Viorst and her children's book *Alexander and the Terrible, Horrible, No Good, Very Bad Day* (New York: Simon and Schuster, 1972).
2. John Whitson, staff writer, "Teen's Gift Surprises, Inspires," *New Hampshire Union Leader*, November 23, 2006. Used by permission, *New Hampshire Union Leader*.

Chapter 2

1. Adapted from Rick Atchley, "When We All Get to Heaven" (sermon, Richland Hills Church of Christ, North Richland Hills, TX, May 25, 2005). Original source unknown.
2. Archibald Naismith, *2400 Outlines, Notes, Quotes, and Anecdotes for Sermons* (Grand Rapids, MI: Baker Book House, 1991), #1063.

Chapter 3

1. Kyle McClure, as told to Chris Lutes, "I Was Being a Hypocrite," *Campus Life*, Nov/Dec 2001, http://www.christianitytoday.com/iyf/2001/novdec/17.20.html. Published by Christianity Today International. Used with permission.
2. Antwone Quenton Fisher, "I Once Was Lost," *Reader's Digest*, July 2001, 81–86.

Chapter 4

1. John Haggai, *How to Win over Worry: A Practical Formula for Successful Living* (Eugene, OR: Harvest House Publishers, 1987), 14.
2. Story of Katie Redner, Suwanee, GA. Used by permission.
3. Haggai, *How to Win over Worry*, 109.
4. Bob Russell, "Reinstated," *Favorite Stories from Bob Russell*, vol. 5, CD-ROM, Southeast Christian Church, Louisville, KY, 2005.
5. William Osler, quoted in Haggai, *How to Win over Worry*, 109.

Chapter 5

1. Mike Wise, "Pushed Beyond the Limit," *Washington Post*, August 30, 2004, D01.
2. Mark Moring, "Why Me?" *Campus Life*, Sept/Oct 2000, http://www.christianitytoday.com/iyf/2000/sepoct/12.72 .html. Published by Christianity Today International. Used with permission.
3. Romans 1:13; 1 Corinthians 11:3; 1 Thessalonians 4:13.
4. F. W. Boreham, *Life Verses: The Bible's Impact on Famous Lives*, Vol. Two (Grand Rapids, MI: Kregel Publications, 1994), 114–55.

Chapter 6

1. Amy Adair, "Didn't God Care?" *Ignite Your Faith*, Sept/Oct 2005, http://www.christianitytoday.com/iyf/2005/sepoct/4.26.html. Used with permission.

Chapter 7

1. Veronica Morris, "Mom for a Day in Mozambique," *Youth with a Mission*, March 13, 2003, http://www.ywam.org/News-Stories/sources/ywam_stories/mom_for_a_day_in_mozambique. Used by permission of Youth with a Mission.
2. Sean Patrick Jackson, "Finding Jesus in the Face of Fear," *Sloppy Noodle*, http://www.sloppynoodle.com/wp/

finding-jesus-in-the-face-of-fearby-sean-patrick-jackson/. Used by permission.

3. Edward Beal, 1041 *Sermon Illustrations, Ideas, and Expositions: Treasury of the Christian World*, ed. A. Gordon Nasby (Grand Rapids, MI: Baker Book House, 1976), 109.

Chapter 8

1. Joanne Brokaw, "Seventh Day Slumber: Outsiders No More." Used with permission. www.joannebrokaw.com.

2. My thanks to my friends John and Lisa Bentley, Michael Landon Jr., and Daniel Sharp for allowing me to share their stories.

3. Katie Wampler, staff writer, "Student Clicks with Seniors, Creates a Way to Help," *Noblesville Daily Times*. Used by permission of the *Noblesville Daily Times*.

Chapter 9

1. "Miracle on Mount Everest," *Dateline NBC*, June 25, 2006, http://www.msnbc.msn.com/id/13543799.

2. Rubel Shelly, "Another Way to Win." Used with permission.

3. Sheila Vaughen, "Niceville Kids Collect Gifts for Iraqi Kids," *Eglin Eagle*, March 26, 2004. Used with permission.

4. Frederick Dale Bruner, *The Christbook: Matthew—A Commentary*, rev. and exp. ed. (Dallas: Word Publishing, 1987), 210.

5. "Great Lakes / South Central Super Teens 2005." © *The Next Step Magazine*, www.nextstepmagazine.com. Used by permission.

6. "Miracle on Mount Everest," *Dateline NBC*.

Chapter 10

1. Austin Atkinson, as told to Christy Heitger-Casbon, "Why Did I Survive?" *Campus Life*, Nov/Dec 2006, http://www.christianitytoday.com/iyf/2006/novdec/10.42.html. Used with permission.

2. Is this your first time to drink from the well of God's

grace? If so, congratulations! You just entered into an eternity-altering relationship. "Whoever accepts and trusts the Son gets in on everything, life complete and forever!" (John 3:36). As you begin your new life, remember three Bs: baptism, Bible, belong. Baptism demonstrates and celebrates our decision to follow Jesus (see 1 Peter 3:21). Regular Bible reading will guide and anchor the soul (see Hebrews 4:12). Belonging to a church family engages us with God's children (see Hebrews 10:25). Ask God to lead you to a group of Christ followers who can celebrate your baptism, help you study the Bible, and serve as a church family.

3. Gary L. Thomas, *Sacred Marriage: What If God Designed Marriage to Make Us Holy More Than to Make Us Happy?* (Grand Rapids, MI: Zondervan, 2000), 46–47.

About the Author

With more than 100 million products in print, Max Lucado is one of America's most widely read authors. He and his wife, Denalyn, live in San Antonio, Texas, where he serves the Oak Hills Church.

SOUR STRESSED CATASTROPHIC
DRAINED AFRAID GUILT J
LOVE INSPIRED PASSIO
GRATEFUL PEACEFUL SOU
STRESSED CATASTROPHIC J
DRAINED AFRAID GUILT LO
INSPIRED PASSION GRATEF
PEACEFUL SOUR STRESSED
SOUR STRESSED CATASTROP
DRAINED AFRAID GUILT J
LOVE INSPIRED PASSIO
GRATEFUL PEACEFUL SOU
STRESSED CATASTROPHIC J